I WAS A KILLER FOR THE HELLS ANGELS

I WAS A
KILLER
FOR THE
HELLS
ANGELS

THE TRUE STORY OF SERGE QUESNEL

PIERRE MARTINEAU
Translated by Jean-Paul Murray

M&S

Original French-language edition © 2002
Les Intouchables and Pierre Martineau
English translation © 2003 McClelland & Stewart Ltd.
and Jean-Paul Murray

National Library of Canada Cataloguing in Publication

Martineau, Pierre, 1965-
I was a killer for the Hells Angels : the story of Serge Quesnel /
Pierre Martineau ; translated by Jean-Paul Murray.

Translation of: Testament d'un tueur des Hells.
ISBN 0-7710-5492-0

1. Quesnel, Serge. 2. Hells Angels–History. 3. Motorcycle gangs–Quebec
(Province)–History. 4. Criminals–Quebec (Province)–Biography.
5. Informers–Quebec (Province)–Biography.
I. Murray, Jean-Paul, 1960- II. Title.

HV6248.Q48M3713 2003   364.1'092   C2003-903535-2

We acknowledge the financial support of the Government of Canada
through the Book Publishing Industry Development Program and that
of the Government of Ontario through the Ontario Media Development
Corporation's Ontario Book Initiative. We further acknowledge
the support of the Canada Council for the Arts and the
Ontario Arts Council for our publishing program.

Typeset in Minion by M&S, Toronto
Printed and bound in Canada

McClelland & Stewart Ltd.
The Canadian Publishers
481 University Avenue
Toronto, Ontario
M5G 2E9
www.mcclelland.com

1 2 3 4 5   07 06 05 04 03

Note

All facts in this book are true,
but some names have been changed.

*To my sons, Nicolas and Anthony,
so that they never cross the
fine line between good and evil*

CONTENTS

FOREWORD

AFTER ALL THOSE YEARS, I can't forget the harm I've done. I'll forever be haunted by memories of making many people suffer and being excessively violent. An enormous weight burdens my existence, and I'll have to carry it for the rest of my life. Not a day goes by when I'm not tormented by recollections of how immoral, inhuman, and insensitive to the misfortunes of others I was.

One of my greatest sorrows is having had so many victims without realizing the seriousness of my actions and their consequences, especially on the members of their families.

You can be sure I feel profound regret and that I'll be looking for a way to redeem myself for the rest of my life.

Allow me very sincerely to ask for your forgiveness.

I only hope that these few lines will help the relatives and friends of my victims. However, I suggest that they close this book right away, since nothing in it will help them understand. The writing of *I Was a Killer for the Hells Angels* was based on statements I made to the police in 1995 and on the numerous interviews I gave to Pierre Martineau. The language used and the events related are not fictionalized. I would have preferred that certain details I'm extremely ashamed of not be mentioned. But Martineau is a journalist by training, and he never lost sight of giving the public complete information. The result is a very blunt book, which reflects the heartless character I was at the time.

Serge Quesnel

PREFACE

SERGE QUESNEL IS THIRTY-THREE years old. Recently, he's lost tens of thousands of dollars in the stock market. Nortel shares have hurt him most. Besides that, he's studying a great deal, trying to make up for lost time – and he's lost a lot of it.

At fifteen, Quesnel preferred hanging around strip bars in downtown Quebec City over going to school. He studied crime, in all its forms. Today, Quesnel is in prison. But you won't know which one. In any case, to ensure his safety, he's often transferred. Quesnel is an informant who sold out the bikers. And not just any bikers: the Hells Angels. *Sold out* is precisely the term. At the time, the informant contract he signed was the largest ever negotiated in the history of Quebec justice. He was awarded $500 a week, tax-free, for fifteen years, for a total of $390,000. Like a wise financier, Quesnel is investing that money. Though he hadn't finished high school and didn't even have a bank account before going to jail at age eighteen, he is now taking university courses. And his marks are amazing.

Quesnel rose through the ranks of the underworld with dazzling speed. He was drafted by the bikers like a hockey player would be by the Montreal Canadiens, by making a name for himself. He beat up a lot of people, and killed a few. Five, to be exact.

Today, Quesnel no longer exercises at the gym, since having strong arms doesn't mean much to him any more. Instead, he's exercising his brain to get ready to manage his new life as an honest citizen. In 2004, when he'll be allowed occasional leave, you might pass him on a street corner. You'll never recognize him. His numerous tattoos have started to be removed – another favour the government granted him in 1995. He'll also be given a new identity, official papers, and a place to live.

Quesnel doesn't disown his past, but he's not proud of it. He sincerely regrets killing five men, all of whom lived off crime. But he feels even more remorse for the families of those men. He wants to mend his ways. Before Quesnel forever drops out of sight, he wants to explain his journey. His life is both spectacular and violent. A killer for the Angels at age twenty-five, Quesnel is today burying his past. Then he will come back to life, as a new man.

Welcome to the world of bikers.

1

THE PATH OF CRIME

THE TIME IS LATE summer 1993. Two young men are getting ready to commit a murder. For the last few months, Serge Quesnel, aged twenty-three, and his friend, aged twenty-two, whose nickname is Nose, have ruled the roost at Donnacona penitentiary. Now they are out and they've decided to enter the "major leagues" of crime together. Their target is Richard Jobin, a forty-four-year-old garage owner who lives in Sainte-Foy. A sturdy fellow, Jobin is a drug dealer who scares a lot of people with his Rottweilers and loud voice. By killing him, Quesnel and Nose will please many people, including Michel "Pit" Caron, a friend of Quesnel and member of the Mercenaires biker club, a group linked to the Quebec City Hells Angels.

On September 9, the two young men head to their victim's mobile home at 1471 des Fougères Street in Sainte-Foy. This is what Quesnel says happened:

"We took a cab and got off about a kilometre and a half from Jobin's house, wanting to make sure the driver couldn't link us to the murder. It was about 10 P.M., and we hadn't taken any drugs or alcohol. We'd borrowed clothes from Martin Naud, a guy I was living with, and slipped them on over the ones we were wearing. If they got stained with Jobin's blood, we could ditch them quickly. The plan was simple. Nose would kill Jobin with his own sawed-off 12 gauge shotgun, which he kept above his kitchen cupboards. The next victim would be mine. Afterwards, we would escape with the garage owner's vehicle.

"But things didn't go exactly as planned. First, Jobin opened the door and asked what we wanted. We told him we had tried to collect money from some guy for the bikers, that he'd fired shots at us, and that we had to hide. We made up a story as he questioned us, and he believed it. He let us in and headed toward the living room. While his back was turned, I grabbed the gun and locked myself in the bathroom. He didn't see me. Nose was talking with Jobin, and I quickly examined the pump-action shotgun, which I thought wasn't loaded. Jobin was getting restless, and was wondering where I was. I hid the weapon and came out. Jobin was obviously nervous. He was pacing the room and went to see if his gun was still in its place. When he noticed it was no longer there, he grew even more nervous.

"Nose lured him into a kind of garage that adjoined the house, where car parts were scattered about. I walked in behind them and grabbed a water pump, which at the time I thought was an alternator. As Jobin was about to leave, I hit him several times on the head, which made a muffled sound. I heard his skull cracking and continued bashing him until he collapsed. He was unconscious, lying face down on the ground, and I could hear his heavy and rapid breathing. Jobin was dying. From the counter, I grabbed a knife with a long blade and gave it to Nose. He drove it into his back, at the height of his heart, drawing the blade along. This time, the sound was disgusting. Then it stopped. Jobin was dead. Once our dirty work was done, we stepped back a little. A piece of toast with peanut butter lay on the counter. Looking at the corpse, Nose grabbed it and ate it."

That's how Quesnel became a murderer. He describes what happened as though talking about a workday, having likely told the story dozens of times to investigators and to the court. At the time, he considered the murder to be a right of passage, his way of proving he was a real criminal, a tough guy. It was the obvious next step for a man who had been "trained" at Donnacona Penitentiary, one of the toughest in the country. In this "school" of brawn and violence, Serge Quesnel had learned a great deal and had made a name for himself. To him, murdering Jobin was simply a means of climbing the underworld ladder more quickly. Because that was the path he'd chosen.

"The arrangements for Jobin's murder weren't very complicated, and we made them practically the same day. We'd purchased surgical gloves in a drugstore and hidden them in the garage of the Mercenaires biker club in Saint-Augustin, along Highway 138, on the outskirts of Quebec City. Jobin was doing 'business' with the Mercenaires as well as with the Rock Machine in Beauport. The biker war hadn't yet started. Jobin had once had a fight with my buddy, Michel 'Pit' Caron. And I knew he would be happy to learn Jobin was dead. Nose and I wanted to prove we didn't attack just anybody. We had a reputation as being daring, and wanted to show it wasn't exaggerated. Violence was part of our everyday life at the time. The two of us collected money for the Mercenaires. We'd call on individuals who owed the club money. This work, which was at times cruel to our 'clients,' provided additional income for Nose and me. We'd get 50 per cent of the amount recovered. But, more often than not, the bikers would tell us to keep everything. We'd sometimes take valuables, though we rarely found any in the slums we visited.

"When we had to collect from someone, we generally reached an agreement with him, and using force wasn't necessary. The usual arrangement was to take money from the guy if he had any, or retrieve all his paycheques or welfare cheques until payment was complete. Sometimes, it was really pitiful. We knew we were taking money intended to feed an entire family. But there was no room for emotion in that world.

"In other circumstances, however, we had to use violence. We were merciless when we caught up with people who hadn't paid up in a long time. Fractures and broken teeth were plentiful. I won't describe all the suffering endured by some men, but, usually, after a good thrashing, the money was paid on time. In short, Nose and I had a reputation as tough guys, and that's what we were."

Serge Quesnel deliberately chose a life of crime, and did so even before leaving Donnacona. While still inside, he told his father that he and his buddy Nose had decided to join the Mercenaires biker club. This would be a preliminary step for the two men, who wanted nothing more than to become Hells Angels.

At the time, the Mercenaires had been in Saint-Augustin for a year, having come from the Beauce region in 1992. Quesnel knew two of the bikers: Michel "Doune" Guérin, the former Mercenaires president who had become a prospect for the Quebec City Hells Angels, and Michel "Pit" Caron, a full-patch member of the Mercenaires. Caron is the man who took care of Quesnel on his release from Donnacona, shortly before Richard Jobin's murder. He sent his brother to pick up Quesnel at the penitentiary and drive him straight to the Quebec City Hells Angels' clubhouse. Caron was there waiting for him while doing his job: watching the comings and goings around the building from the observation room.

"The trip from Donnacona to Saint-Nicolas, where the Angels' clubhouse was located, seemed very brief. I felt restless by the time we reached the impressive red-and-white building. My buddy Pit was waiting for me at the entrance. The clubhouse door was bulletproof, of course, and I couldn't miss the famous winged death's head painted on it. It was the symbol of the organization's power. Pit motioned me to follow him inside, where several bikers were chatting. The atmosphere was relaxed and music was playing softly. The Angels were sitting around the bar. After Pit introduced me to them, we headed to the observation room. The place was clean and contained several objects bearing the Angels' crest. There were slogans as well, and photographs of every Angels chapter on earth. From Australia to North America through Europe, the Hells Angels are everywhere. It was impressive.

"Pit was happy to see me again, and we talked a little about the old days. I'd known Pit since I was a teenager. He was a little older than I was, and thought highly of me for some reason. When I met him, I was a petty hoodlum, a thief, hanging around a schoolyard in Ancienne-Lorette while he worked at the Robert-Giffard hospital in Quebec City. Over time, he'd managed to put together an important drug distribution network, which allowed him to earn a lot of money for himself and his bosses. Now he suggested that I become one of his dealers. The attractive part of the offer was that Nose already belonged to Pit's team. All I had to do was accept. I had to earn money. Pit told me how he operated before giving me a few hundred dollars to tide me over. Afterwards, his brother drove me to the probation office where I was scheduled to meet my parole officer. The meeting lasted a few minutes, and I was told I was never to consume alcohol or drugs or to associate with anyone with a criminal record. That night, I celebrated my release by touring the bars on Grande-Allée Street, with all my honest friends!"

Shortly after his release, Quesnel ran into Martin Naud, a guy he knew in high school. Naud was a drug dealer, and he immediately agreed to join Quesnel's new network. This twenty-five-year-old man had already been in trouble with the law, and the police knew he was associated with the Mercenaires. They often showed up at his mobile home on Sainte-Famille Street in the Laurentien neighbourhood of Sainte-Foy, but they never managed to catch him. After chatting briefly, the two young criminals decided to live together, and Quesnel moved in with Naud that day.

"Although the drug network's clientele was continually increasing, I had another plan in mind: attacking an armoured vehicle with Nose and two other accomplices, Mario and Jeff, both of whom had also just been released from Donnacona. We robbed three or four banks to get some practice. One day, Mario, Nose, and I robbed the Banque Nationale on Masson Boulevard. While Nose was in the car, Mario and I, masked and armed, entered the bank. I ordered the manager to hang up the phone and kept an eye on the employees while Mario filled his bag. We quickly left the premises and went over to Mario's place, in Beauport, to split up the money. We'd robbed $18,000. The following week, Nose, Mario, Jeff, and I decided to rob the same bank again since we'd managed to get a lot of money the first time. Nose and I stayed in the car. We were armed with a sawed-off 12 gauge shotgun and a .38. After a few minutes, Mario and Jeff came out running. As they climbed into the car, they said there wasn't much money so we immediately decided to do another bank. We hit the Banque

Nationale on First Avenue in Charlesbourg. In all, we got about $4,000. It wasn't a very big day.

"Nose, Mario, Jeff, and I did several more heists, all of which took place with lightning speed. We'd steal a vehicle and drive up to the bank, each of us carrying a pump-action shotgun. Two of us would stay in the car while the other two walked into the bank, yelling, 'Holdup!' If I were the one to jump over the counter to get the money, my accomplice would keep an eye on customers. Meanwhile, outside, the other two would keep the cops at bay. I preferred going inside; time passed more quickly.

"We were very dangerous at the time. We had no qualms about using our weapons. We'd just been released from Donnacona and none of us wanted to go back. We didn't want to stand trial. If we had to, we wanted the trial to be in the street. Following our heists, we'd go to Mario's place to count the money. It was impressive to see so many fifty- and hundred-dollar bills on the bed. We used the cash to buy weapons for our planned attack on the armoured vehicle. But Mario and Jeff were arrested while trying out those weapons in a Val-Bélair sandpit, and got a few more years in jail as a result. Nose and I put an end to this string of robberies and went back to our drug business. The armoured-vehicle heist was put on ice.

"Then I fell in love with Nose's sister, Chantal. This was at the end of the summer, in August. I first met her while I was in Donnacona, when she'd come to visit her brother. But I'd been unable to catch her eye then. Now it was different, and from the outset, things went very well between us. She was really beautiful, tall, with blonde hair and green eyes. The ideal woman. She didn't ask too many questions either, or worry about petty details. She was nice."

When he was with Chantal, Quesnel was able to relax. He was less aggressive and enjoyed spending time at her home with her. Since Chantal's brother, Nose, had a criminal record, Quesnel managed to have the clause preventing him from associating with criminals removed. His relationship with Chantal allowed him to do so, and he took full advantage of it.

"It was good for me to come home and spend as much time as possible with my girlfriend. I occasionally felt like finding a job to earn an honest living, to pull out, to have a little less action. But it's hard to break old habits. Besides, Nose and I were a solid unit. He'd always supported me, in the pen and on the outside. Since we had to eat, we continued our heists. But we wanted more. We didn't want to spend the rest of our lives committing small-time robberies to feed ourselves. We knew that a murder would guarantee us an interesting 'career' in crime."

Quesnel knew his first victim well, as he had once sold drugs for him. He was fifteen when he met Richard Jobin. He was already robbing convenience stores and met Jobin when he sold him some cigarettes he'd stolen. Then he started selling PCP and cocaine for Jobin, dealing two to three ounces a week with the help of as many as five guys who worked for him. Jobin was a tough guy who liked to flex his muscles. By choosing him as a target, Quesnel and Nose were showing they really weren't afraid of him – or anyone.

"I was surprised about my feelings after the murder. I felt nothing. I'd just executed a man, and I was keeping my cool. This gave me confidence for the career I was planning. It's as though the penitentiary, and everything I experienced there, had prepared me to kill without a problem. It was an accomplishment. In killing that man, I got an adrenalin rush, but I never lost control. I was totally lucid. My partner remained very calm as well. Nose and I had become killing machines. And we knew the ropes. Once the murder was committed, we took the time to erase all possible fingerprints. Jobin had an impressive collection of weapons in his home: cross-bows, firearms, and other collector's items. Nose wanted to steal an AK-47, but I wouldn't let him, telling him that our visit had only one purpose and that we'd achieved it. Killing someone and then stealing from him is frowned on in the underworld. It's referred to as a *burn*.

"We left Jobin's site calmly, still disguised, and made our way to some nearby woods, where we removed our overgarments. We hid the clothes inside a cord of wood, planning to burn them later, then we walked for about two kilometres to a bar, where we called a cab to drive us to the Mercenaires' clubhouse. Pit was happy when we told him the big guy was dead. Nose and I were proud, having managed to kill the local terror without using a gun. We burned our shoes in a forty-five-gallon drum in the yard of the biker clubhouse. I then filled a container with gasoline and we went back to burn the clothes we'd stashed. I was sure they were bloodstained, and wanted to leave no evidence. Once we'd done this, I returned to the Mercenaires' clubhouse and went to bed."

Jobin's body was found the next day by one of his employees, who called the police. Later, perhaps to put himself to a test, Serge Quesnel went back to Jobin's and spoke with the employee. He listened carefully, wanting to know if the police had found any clues, but learned nothing. Quesnel then returned to the house he shared with Martin Naud.

"I'd just returned to Naud's place and was watching TV in the living room when two policemen showed up at the front door to talk to Naud. They wanted to question him since, according to witnesses, he'd been the last person to speak to Jobin. Naud told them where he'd been at the time of the crime. His story was credible, since he had nothing to do with the murder. One of the detectives knew me and asked how I was doing. In a relaxed manner, I told him I was doing very well. The conversation was brief because, at that precise moment, the TV newscast began. From the start of the program, the topic was the murder in Sainte-Foy. The two detectives sat on the couch beside me to watch the news. The situation was comical. The two officers investigating the murder were seated beside the killer, listening to the news report with him! I felt like laughing but knew that I couldn't. The two officers were proud of being seen in the report. They commented on the image they projected on TV."

Possibly more to set his mind to rest than from a sense of duty, one of the policemen asked Quesnel if he knew anything about Jobin's murder. The young man answered quietly that the officer would have to speak to his lawyer. Quesnel was sure of himself. At least, that was the impression he gave.

"I realized I was probably among the suspects, but this left me indifferent. I didn't worry about it, knowing the work had been well done and that there was no evidence to link me to it. I just went about my business. Nose and I robbed a few more banks, while continuing to collect for the bikers. This work was sometimes pathetic. Some men really got good beatings. I remember this one guy sitting at the end of his kitchen table beside his twelve pack of beer. He was a little cheeky. We broke every bottle over his head while threatening him. He was bleeding a lot. I think he paid up. Another time, Nose gave me a good laugh. The guy we had to collect from had a waterbed and Nose wanted to take it to teach him a lesson. He tried to lift the bed and cried out, 'That's really heavy! How'd he bring it up here?' I was dying of laughter. But we didn't spend all our time collecting money. There were also parties and drugs. I often took PCP, coke, hash, and alcohol."

In the weeks following Jobin's murder, Quesnel was more violent than ever. He was nearly always armed, spending more and more time with his roommate, Martin Naud.

"One night, Martin asked me to go with him to a corn roast a friend of his was organizing. When I arrived, I spotted Gonzo, one of my former drug pushers, who'd owed me $1,000 for several months. Gonzo was supposed to bring me the money while I was at Donnacona, but had never done so. I'd tried to find him afterwards, but he was in hiding. When I saw him that night, I asked him to follow me behind the house and I beat him with a revolver grip. Pit Caron had given me the gun. I hit him on the face and head until he fell, then kicked him repeatedly. Once he was really punch-drunk, I leaned over him and told him to pay me very quickly. After that, I went back to join the other guests and partied. The remainder of the evening was fun."

A few days later, Quesnel decided to leave Naud's house and move in with his mother, who lived on de la Randonnée Street in Quebec City. The reason: Naud had decided to stop selling drugs for Quesnel and Nose. He was still dealing for the Quebec City Hells Angels, but through another network. Quesnel and Nose tried to dissuade Naud from leaving them, but he had already made up his mind. During the previous weeks, he had often gone out with the two young killers. Now and again, he had even replaced Quesnel and had gone with Nose on collection runs for the bikers. For a while, Quesnel and his buddy had even considered making him into a good "soldier," the bikers' term for an accomplished criminal.

"We wanted Martin to get some experience and become a little more violent. We wanted to find out if he had the nerves to be involved at a higher level. I think Nose told him details about Jobin's murder, which cost Martin very dearly. I was disappointed when he told me he was leaving. It bothered me. I really liked him. He was a good guy, and a lot of fun. Nose, for his part, couldn't stomach his departure. He may have been afraid of Martin, of being turned in by him. Martin had been asking a lot of questions about Jobin's death. Perhaps he wanted to leave because he was afraid of us. Anyhow, Nose was growing more paranoid about Martin. And I also thought Martin talked about Jobin too often. He seemed sure that we'd killed him."

On the night of October 20, 1993, about a month after Jobin's murder, Quesnel and Nose were at a friend's place on Fifth Street in Quebec City. By this time, the two men were inseparable. That night, they drank a lot and snorted a few lines of PCP, a particularly harsh drug. At one point, Nose scribbled a few words on a piece of paper and handed it to his friend.

"He gave me the note. He'd written, 'Tonight, we'll kill Martin Naud.' I didn't ask any questions and we left. We hadn't said a word. I didn't challenge Nose's decision. To me, it was as simple as that. Nose had made a decision and so I had to help him. He'd always been there for me. At Donnacona, I'd always been able to count on his support. He'd often risked being injured for my sake. We went down the building's stairs. As we were walking, I asked Nose if we had to kill Martin, and he said yes. We took my car, a 1987 Buick Century, because Nose's was in the garage. My mind was a little muddled, likely due to the PCP.

"We drove to the Quebec Inn Hotel, where I had parked my car. On the way, we didn't speak about Martin Naud at all. We were already very cautious, wary of microphones, and I never spoke of criminal activities inside a car. Since Jobin's murder, we'd been taking all necessary precautions. We wouldn't talk about it in a house or any other place likely to be bugged. When we got out of the car, it was very late. As we walked to Naud's, we quickly drew up a plan. Because of the agreement we had, it was my turn to kill Naud. I had to put my feelings aside. I programmed myself and was on automatic pilot. We knocked on his door, but there was no answer. The door wasn't locked, and we went in. Martin was sleeping in his bed, at the other end of the house, with his little dog. We opened the door, then turned on the light. Martin woke up with a start.

"'What's going on?' he asked.

"'Get up, we need your help,' I said.

"'How come you walk into people's homes without knocking?'

"'The door wasn't locked, and we need your help. We'll take your car and you'll have to come with us.'

"'I have to be in court tomorrow,' said Naud, getting dressed.

"'It won't take long, and you'll be in fine shape tomorrow.'

"Naud was nervous. I could feel it. While he was in his bedroom getting dressed, Nose was in the living room, taking the laces out of his shoes. Martin walked into the living room and asked Nose what he was doing. Nose didn't answer. Martin turned toward me and I then gave him a bear hug, to pin his arms. That's when Nose did his dirty work, strangling him with his own shoelace. Martin was struggling and I let him go. But Nose was holding him tightly. Martin grabbed Nose's hands, driving his nails into his skin, even though Nose was wearing gloves. Meanwhile, I was looking for something to finish him off, a knife or some such thing. I spotted a pair of scissors. Martin was weakening and Nose dropped him. Martin had lost consciousness, and it was my turn to kill. I grabbed the orange-handled scissors and plunged them into his eye, trying to get at the brain. Then, I pulled out the scissors and slit his throat. I wanted to make sure he was dead.

"It was very bad. The place was really awful to look at. On the floor, lying in a pool of his blood, was a friend I'd just killed for no reason. I had to conceal my emotions and just get on with the job. I felt I was on a mission, as though I were at war. Nose caught Martin's dog and put him in his cage. Since I had been living in this house until recently, we decided to set fire to it because my fingerprints were everywhere. I found a bottle of rubbing alcohol in the bathroom. I emptied it on Martin and set fire to him, thinking the house would go up as well. Then we left. Heading back to the car, we spotted a police cruiser moving very slowly along the road. It was likely a routine patrol, but we were nervous and ran. Nose lost a shoe. Once back in my car, the tension went down a notch. I drove Nose to his place on des Sables Street in Limoilou, and I went back to my mother's apartment. She was away that night."

Martin Naud died young. Yet, in the hours following the news of his murder, one of his close relatives told the media that his death was a deliverance to his family. Naud had spent time in a halfway house as a teenager and was always trying to get money from his parents, forever trying to manipulate them. But this didn't make his murder, like Jobin's, any more unacceptable.

For Insp. Pierre Frenette, an officer with the Sûreté du Québec, also known as the Quebec Police Force (QPF), who worked on Serge Quesnel's case for more than two years – acting as his handler throughout all the legal proceedings – Quesnel's two first murders were monumental blunders.

"They were major mistakes on his part. Two acts of folly. He committed them just to make a name for himself, to climb the underworld ladder quickly, to impress. He was more animal than man when he killed that guy. It was the fastest way he knew to become a major-league criminal. He wanted to establish himself as quickly as possible and make money. That's the method he chose."

Back in his mother's apartment, Quesnel tried not to think too much about what had just happened. Then he noticed the bloodstains on his clothes.

"I was wearing jeans and a black sweatshirt. Printed on the sweatshirt were two motorcycles ridden by skeletons, along with the slogan, in red, Support Your Crew, Quebec City. I threw out the clothes. Despite the horrible crime I'd committed, I managed to fall asleep. The next day, Nose and I went back to the vicinity of Naud's house, trying to find the shoe Nose had lost, which could prove a very important piece of evidence. We didn't find it, but I noticed that Naud's house hadn't burned down. Later that day, we went to the home of our friend on Fifth Street, where we'd been the previous night, and watched our first newscast of the day. When the journalist began talking about Martin, I joked that he must have committed suicide. But my joking quickly gave way to fear. The journalist gave an impressive list of the details the police had revealed to the media. I was nervous and had a bad premonition."

Obviously, the killing had made a lot of noise. The murder was despicable, and the police were speaking of carnage. It was the second homicide in two months, and the gruesome details were making headlines. The victims, Jobin and Naud, not only knew each other, they both had contacts with bikers.

"I was pretty shaken up. This was the only thing people were talking about in Quebec City, and the media weren't letting up, disclosing all the troubling details.

The cops were hinting that Naud's murderer had probably lived at his place and that he was a former Donnacona inmate – they were just falling short of naming me. Part of me was ashamed and remorseful when details of the murder were circulated, but the other part felt respected by the underworld. It was strange. The underworld feared us and the cops were watching me. Pit Caron was freaking out, wondering what his bosses, the Hells Angels, would think of the murder. One thing was certain, however: the cops were targeting Nose and me. On TV, a witness who lived near Martin's place was saying he had seen Martin and his roommate fighting a few days prior to the crime. He described the roommate as being a tough guy from Donnacona with tears tattooed on his face."

Quesnel had tattooed those tears on his face when he was sixteen years old, while he was staying at a youth centre. One night, after taking a lot of drugs, probably PCP, he had soaked carbon paper in water to make ink and fashioned a needle from two paper clips. In intense pain, no doubt – he doesn't remember – Quesnel managed to tattoo tears under both eyes. His mother cried when she saw what he had done, and his father was staggered.

"When I saw Serge with tattoos on his face, I was worried. I didn't like it at all. However, I was wondering if he'd chosen tears because he had regrets. Why tears? And on his face, moreover. I thought it could mean several things."

But his son now had more important things to care about than the various interpretations given to his tattoos.

"I was stunned by the neighbour's testimony. I thought everyone knew it was me. Besides, the cops were playing on my nerves. One morning while I was sleeping at my mother's place, a few days after Martin's murder, I was woken by a helicopter flying very close to the house. I looked out the window and saw it was a QPF helicopter. It wasn't the Sainte-Foy police who were looking for us, it was the QPF! I was getting more and more nervous, and couldn't move since the cops were watching us closely. When driving a car, I would spend all my time looking in the rear-view mirror. If I had any doubts, I accelerated, and if the car behind me did the same, I knew it was the cops. This happened quite often. I would go into a shopping centre through one door and exit through another. Often, a friend would be waiting for me with his car, and I'd regain my freedom for a few hours. I liked to surprise the cops who were tailing me. At times, when I saw them in their parked cars, waiting for me to come out of some building, I'd go over and knock on the side of their vehicle. I liked to bother them, to show them how badly they were doing their jobs.

They'd often pretend they weren't there on my account, and I'd get real pleasure out of exposing them."

While the vise was slowly tightening on Quesnel and his partner, there was a lot of commotion at the Angels' clubhouse in Quebec City. The bikers were furious. As a PCP dealer, Naud had earned a lot of money for the organization. Everyone in the underworld knew that Quesnel and Nose were the killers. Jim, a full-patch member of the Angels, ordered Pit Caron to kill the two of them. But Caron felt that he couldn't carry out the order and tried to find another solution.

"Pit wanted Nose and me to leave," Quesnel says. "He said he could feel the heat. Obviously, he didn't say he'd been ordered to kill us. But I refused. To leave would be to admit guilt. I didn't want to do that. Also, I was in love with Chantal. My girlfriend didn't know I was Naud's murderer. She may have suspected it, but I hadn't told her a thing. A few days after the murder, while Chantal and I were in a restaurant, she started reading a newspaper article that mentioned Naud's death. I was ashamed and felt awful. The article, which I'd read, related disgusting details. I was anxious for her to move on to something else."

The pressure on the two killers was enormous. The underworld was talking about the crime; police were everywhere. Eventually Quesnel decided to see his lawyer.

"When I reached my lawyer's office, one of his associates greeted me before going to get him. On seeing me, my lawyer said, 'As soon as I saw the news, I knew it was you!' But he immediately reassured me by promising to defend me if there were charges. Then, laughing, he suggested I return to Sainte-Foy if I had other murders to commit. In his view, the investigators there were idiots, and I wouldn't have any problems."

Things were starting to get serious. Even Quesnel's parole officer, whom he met every week, mentioned the suspicions hanging over him. Too many people around him were dying, she said. Quesnel told her he was glad not to have been at Naud's place on the night of the murder, since he might have been done in as well. Quesnel was a compulsive liar. That night, even though he wasn't allowed to, he went to the Laurentien bar with one of his brothers-in-law.

"I was trying to relax by drinking quite a bit. We were sitting at a table, listening to a rock group, when a drunk guy came over and started to bother me. The guy was acting heavy and getting worked up. I told him to leave us alone and he told me off. So I asked him to follow me outside and, once there, I punched him in the face. It was enough to stop him. My friend and I then left and went to a strip bar. Thirty or so minutes later, the Sainte-Foy police arrived. I was charged with assault and ended up in a cell at the police station. At that point,

I was sure I'd see QPF investigators arrive any minute. I was convinced they'd ask me about the two murders committed over the last two months. But nothing happened. The cops took my fingerprints and then brought me before a judge. I couldn't get over it. No doubt thinking they were impressing me, the cops charged me with a second assault. Several weeks earlier, I'd taken part in a bar fight, where Nose manhandled a hulking brute who'd laughed at us. At the high point of the altercation, I neutralized a friend of the guy Nose was fighting with. I also punched him. Nose wouldn't settle for so little and beat the guy savagely. So I was charged in relation to that incident."

Quesnel was taken before the court, but his first victim didn't show up. This happened twice. At the third hearing, the man appeared in handcuffs; he had been arrested for theft. He said he'd been hit by Quesnel, who was sentenced almost immediately. As for the later fight, the man Quesnel hit couldn't remember a thing. Nonetheless, the court found Quesnel guilty of being an accomplice.

"I was anxious to leave the court, feeling I was lucky. I didn't want the guy to regain his memory and think I was getting off lightly."

Quesnel received a ten-month sentence and was immediately sent back to Donnacona. As for Nose, the beating he gave cost him dearly: the judge sentenced him to four years in the penitentiary. Of course, both men would leave prison long before the end of their terms. In all, Quesnel had been out of Donnacona for three months, during which he killed two men, committed three robberies, and beat up some thirty people.

"Now and then, I'd think about my actions and the harm I was doing. I even thought of my victims' families. But I'd quickly put aside those regrets. I wasn't ready to change, and so I suppressed my feelings very deeply. My reputation in the underworld was now established, and I was known both in and out of prison. I was twenty-three years old, and the values I'd been taught were on the back burner. At that point, I could see only one path, and that was crime. I couldn't imagine doing anything else. There was nothing else for me, and the men I was mixing with were the worst criminals. The prison world was my home."

◎

The two murders Quesnel committed in 1993 were, at that point, the culmination of his life as a criminal. He had been hanging around the underworld since he was a teenager. He had begun his criminal career with petty shoplifting with high-school friends – then he moved on to purse-snatching and robbing houses and banks. Drugs and alcohol were a constant in his life. He thought only of having fun and went to school only because he had to. Yet, he never failed a school year. His parents, who have been separated since he was four years old, couldn't reason with him. According to his father, Serge was a restless child.

"He was turbulent. Always had to be moving. If there was a button, he had to press it. He wanted to discover everything all at once. He was curious and enterprising, and had lots of energy to burn. Definitely a turbulent child. I think he never accepted that his mother and I were separated. When he was about twelve, he did all he could to get us back together. Nor could he accept that his mother made a fresh start, that she had other men in her life."

"As a child, I moved often," says Quesnel. "My mother liked to change scenery. I saw my father regularly. Then when I went back to my mother's place, she wouldn't know how to reason with me. For the first year of high school I went to the Saint-Louis school, in Loretteville. I didn't mind it. I'd smoke pot and hash with other students and we'd anger the teachers. I couldn't stand authority. I especially remember this one woman; we loved to drive her up the wall. I don't recall what she taught, but we were so unruly that she'd often leave the classroom in tears. My attitude, however, did get me into trouble. One day, during an ethics class, while I was loitering at my desk with other students, the teacher slapped me in the face. The man was probably fed up with me. I froze. I was insulted. I was angry with him for a long time. Once my criminal career was well underway, I think I would have beaten him up had I met him. But at that point, nothing was going well. I continued going to school, but was flunking more and more courses. I preferred going to the arcade with my friends."

No doubt worried by her son's behaviour and resolved to teach him a lesson, Quesnel's mother transferred him to a private school, Mont-Saint-Sacrement, a boys' school where activities were well structured. But he hated it, making only enough effort to pass the year, after which he returned to a public high school.

"I ended up with several guys I knew, and started hanging around with gangs. We planned robberies, home robberies in particular. It lasted a few months. Afterwards, I moved in with my father, in Sainte-Foy. I attended the technical school, taking technical drawing courses. Frédéric Faucher was in my class."

Frédéric Faucher also went on to become a major criminal. Head of the Quebec Rock Machine, he merged his biker group with the Bandidos, a world power in crime, comparable to the Hells Angels. Faucher, now in his early thirties, is an explosives expert. Since December 2000, he has been serving an eleven-year prison sentence for several crimes. He pleaded guilty to twenty-eight charges, half of which were for dealing cocaine. Faucher also admitted to committing seven bombings between 1996 and 1997 during the biker war. Judge Pierre Verdon emphasized, while delivering his sentence, that the accused had to be imprisoned for reasons of public security. According to the police investigation, Faucher's cocaine and PCP network earned him a quarter-million dollars a month. He will be paroled in 2008.

Adolescence was an extremely turbulent time for Quesnel. Even his brother, who is a few years older, couldn't reason with him. Serge came home later and later each night. At school, he was failing more and more courses. His friends were all that counted.

"He no longer made any effort at school," his father says. "He was distracted and didn't study. I often told him to pay attention at school, but he only did as he pleased. He was very easily influenced by his friends."

"We robbed houses and businesses, spending the money in bars," Quesnel says. "We also discovered underground bars. Sometimes, I'd come home at 6 A.M., when my mother was up, getting ready to go to work. She was increasingly discouraged with me. When I was at school, policemen often came over to question me about all sorts of robberies. I was also into purse-snatching. I'd start to run, grab the purse of a woman in front of me, then scurry away. One day, I stole the purse of the mother of a tough guy from my school. He was a few years older than me and I heard he was looking for the snatcher. So I went into hiding for a while. The money I stole allowed me to buy drugs. I stopped doing this kind of robbery when I realized it wasn't really fair to the women we were robbing. Also, they screamed so much that it was frightening. Then I was caught and charged with theft and serious assault before the youth court. The assault had occurred a few months earlier. My mother had given me a BB gun. One day, when I'd done PCP, for kicks I took shots at two mentally handicapped people who lived nearby. I opened my bedroom window and fired a few BBs at them. I couldn't tell if I was hitting them because the two men were continually scratching themselves. When the cops came over to my house, I felt really ashamed. The father of the two men had called them. He'd even taken pictures of me leaning out the window, with the gun in my hands."

In this world of young toughs, Quesnel climbed the ladder of crime quickly. He even managed to set up a network of house robbers that also involved three taxi drivers who picked up the young people and bought the things they liked from among the stolen goods.

"Sometimes, during those robberies, I'd get a shock. One day, when I was in a large house, I came face to face with a very old lady. I had the jewellery box in my hands. The lady kept repeating, 'What's going on? What's going on?' As I was about to run away, a man came into the house and we had a scuffle. Another time, I ran into a large dog and had to knock him out with my crowbar."

During this period, Quesnel was holding down his first and last job as assistant cook in a Sainte-Foy restaurant. He kept it for two weeks. His brother and his girlfriend were already working in the restaurant and so he knew the man who hired him. Since he was scheduled to appear before the youth court, Quesnel had been advised to find work to make a good impression on the judge.

"My boss did cocaine, and I supplied him. So he let me do as I pleased. I loitered around much more than I worked, and was constantly looking for trouble. If cops came to eat, I took care of them, discreetly spitting in their food. Everything was an excuse to have fun and fool around. But I didn't work in that restaurant very long."

The young man started stealing cars, at first to learn how to drive, then to go to school. And, at age seventeen, he got into armed robbery.

"I was always stoned when committing robberies. I'd take a gun, a knife, or a baseball bat, threatening the person behind the counter, leaving with more or less considerable amounts."

Quesnel's mother was at a loss to know how to bring her son back from a life of crime. She tried everything, from discussions to threats, without success. She even told the cops who arrested her son to "shake him up" to make him understand. But the teenager just wouldn't listen. Her patience exhausted, Quesnel's mother resorted to drastic measures: she placed him in a centre for troubled youth for one month. Quesnel ended up in Tilly, surrounded by young criminals.

"It wasn't a place to send a young person, though I understood my mother's reasons for doing so. I was out of control. There, I met lots of guys I'd see again later. They were young delinquents at the time. I felt like I was in jail. A social worker had convinced my mother to send me to Tilly. That's where I realized I'd have a career in crime. One day, when a teacher asked me where I thought I'd be in 2000, I realized I'd probably be in jail. Crime was all I knew. I was attracted by the idea of making easy money."

"There was nothing more we could do to stop him from going into crime," says his father. "I tried a few times, back then, to bring him back to the straight and narrow, but he wouldn't listen. He alone knew what was good for him."

So Quesnel continued his apprenticeship as a criminal. On leaving Tilly, he went back to robbing and hanging out with all kinds of shady characters. With a friend named Éric, he travelled to the Rivière-du-Loup region to rob houses and businesses, service stations in particular.

"It was relatively easy. We'd go to a garage. My buddy would be driving. He'd fill up and ask the attendant to check the oil and the tire pressure. Meanwhile, I'd go over to the counter, open the cash register, and take the money. Then we'd take off. One night, however, the cops collared us. We'd partied in a small Rivière-du-Loup bar following a few heists, but one of our victims had given a detailed description of our vehicle. On the way back, in the middle of the night, the police stopped us. The vehicle was filled with stolen goods. I'd just turned eighteen."

Quesnel was sentenced to a year in jail. He was sent to Orsainville, a provincial facility on the outskirts of Quebec City. This was his first time inside a detention centre. It was a difficult moment for Quesnel's father.

"I couldn't take it. I was overwhelmed, very sad. I felt powerless. As a parent, you blame yourself. I'm convinced that the separation from my wife played an important part in his descent into hell."

"Your family isn't what turns you into a criminal, it's the company you keep," says Insp. Pierre Frenette of the QPF. "Even if Quesnel had the best parents in the world, once out on the street he followed only his own rules. He was hanging out on the street, taking drugs, and was easily influenced. He kept bad company and went astray."

Unlike most people who end up in jail at such a young age, Quesnel didn't feel out of place. Having heard a lot about it, he already knew this world and its inhabitants quite well. At Orsainville, he met Nose.

"I was with the other inmates, in the prison yard. Suddenly, a guy who was about thirty years old started bothering Nose. He was seated, hands behind his head, with his legs on a picnic table, looking at Nose and laughing. Nose grabbed a baseball bat, ran up to the other inmate, and began hitting him everywhere with all his strength. He was really mad. The other guy got a real good beating. Both his arms were broken. I'd just discovered Nose."

In order to spend the least time possible in jail and serve only a sixth of his sentence, Quesnel asked to be transferred to the Ferme de l'Espoir, a rehabilitation centre for delinquent drug addicts located in Saint-Isidore, a town in the Beauce region. The strategy didn't work for long. Quesnel couldn't have cared less about the therapy he was offered and, worse, was caught taking drugs. He was sent back to Orsainville, finally serving eight months in jail. He stayed on the outside for only a short time before he was caught for robbing convenience stores. He was also charged for breaking the terms of his probation. His lawyer suggested a sentence of two years less a day, but Quesnel asked for two years. The difference seems minor, but it determines whether the sentence will be served in a provincial detention centre or a federal prison. Quesnel insisted on going to a federal prison.

"I wanted to go to the penitentiary to continue my education. I also wanted better prison conditions. In federal institutions, there are TVs everywhere and conditions are better."

Quesnel entered this new prison environment as a young adult, and would age prematurely in the years that followed. He got the education he really wanted, the kind that doesn't come with textbooks. He was parachuted into the world of crime. All he had to do was watch and listen to his "teachers."

2

DONNACONA

DONNACONA, a town of some five-thousand residents, is about a twenty-minute drive from Quebec City. Many people consider the penitentiary in this small town to be the toughest in the country. It houses over 350 prisoners serving sentences of more than two years – terms that are often extended because of offences inmates commit during their detention. Sixty or so of them are serving life sentences. They will die inside those walls.

Serge Quesnel arrived at Donnacona on December 10, 1989, at the age of nineteen, without the least apprehension. His two-year sentence stretched to nearly four years behind bars since he racked up no fewer than twenty-eight charges while in prison.

"I had no reason to be afraid, as nobody had a grudge against me at Donnacona. I understood the law of the place: walk straight, mind your own business, and don't let anyone step on your toes. I ran into three of my friends when I arrived: Éric, my accomplice in the Rivière-du-Loup robberies, Stéphane, whom I'd known at the drop-in centre, and Carl. Everything went smoothly in the first weeks. I was rather quiet, going about my business."

Then, one morning, a new inmate arrived: Yves Plamondon, nicknamed Colosse (Colossus in English). His moniker was no exaggeration: he had the physique of a bodybuilder. Before being transferred to Donnacona he'd been in an Ontario prison. Colosse Plamondon, forty years old, was a dealer for Montreal's Dubois brothers and was given a life sentence in 1986 after being convicted of three murders.

"I didn't know Plamondon when he arrived, but I saw that the other inmates had a lot of respect for him. He was described as being dangerous, but I never saw him be violent. He had his gang, and would get the others to do the work. He associated in particular with Robert Péruta, who came to the penitentiary a few weeks later."

Péruta was thirty-eight years old at the time. He'd been serving a thirty-year sentence since 1977 for several attempted murders. In 1989, he attracted a lot of attention for murdering another prisoner, Claude Péloquin, with two accomplices. Péloquin had been found in a pool of blood, his throat pierced by a broom handle whose tip had been sharpened into a point. Péruta had made headlines in 1994. He was officially divorced and wanted to remarry. As he couldn't get a civil wedding inside the penitentiary, he managed to get permission to be married in the Quebec City courthouse. Under tight escort, wearing handcuffs and ankle chains, he married twenty-nine-year-old Marie-Anna Simard. Police were everywhere, and the numerous journalists who wanted to cover the event were kept out of the room. Fifteen or so people surrounded the lovebirds. Colosse Plamondon had asked for permission to attend the wedding as a witness for the groom. It was denied. Following the short ceremony, the newlyweds headed back to the penitentiary, to the famous "nuptial" trailer. Many years later, Quesnel would be ordered to kill Péruta on his release from jail. He was resented for his behaviour behind bars.

"As soon as Colosse arrived at Donnacona, I could see the influence he had. He quickly mobilized a number of people. At the time, there was an escape plan afoot involving several inmates. The guys had a spectacular plan of digging a tunnel under the yard in the middle of winter. They wanted to cut a hole into the sewer pipe that ran beside the ice rink. The snow gave cover to the guys going into the tunnel after they'd broken the cement covering the manhole. Once inside, they had to saw through several metal grilles. The guys – and there were many of them – took turns while two other prisoners stood watch near the entrance. I didn't hang around with the gang that had come up with the plan, but all the prisoners knew what was going on. One day, the guards discovered the plot. All the guys inside the tunnel were arrested and immediately transferred to Montreal's 'super-maximum' security facility, the Special Handling Unit. I pointed out to the two guys who'd stood watch that they were lucky not to have been caught by the guards. One of them didn't understand and thought I was insinuating it was fishy that they hadn't been arrested. His name was André, and he was a dangerous character. He started bawling me out in the common room, in front of other inmates. The other guy, the one I'd spoken to, was called Marco. He'd deliberately distorted my words. Colosse was a witness to the scene. Following André's fit, he came over to tell me not to let myself be pushed around.

"And that's what I did. Though I was much younger than Marco, I couldn't accept such an insult from him. In prison, not talking back is a sign of weakness. I devised a simple plan. Since Marco played hockey, I figured the best place to attack him was at the exit of the building where players put on their equipment. On game night, while the guys were dressing before going onto the ice,

I walked through the locker room and headed for the rink. Under my coat, I had an eighteen-inch iron bar. I hid under the portico leading outside. It was dark. I was sweating and nervous, but had no choice. I had to act. I had to make sure the guy was sufficiently beaten up that the guards would have to transfer him to another detention centre. I soon spotted Marco walking toward the portico, wearing skates and a helmet. When he walked through the doorway, I dashed out and hit him with all my strength in the forehead, right below the helmet. He spun around and went down on all fours. He tried to get up, but his skates were rubbing against a metal grille. I stood paralyzed, watching him. After struggling for several seconds, he managed to stand up, looking at me with glazed eyes, before heading inside, where he collapsed near the guards. He was immediately carried out on a stretcher. When the bell rang, at 8 P.M., to let in the prisoners, the guards were joking, saying, "They're playing rough tonight." Naturally, I was proud, having just proved my worthiness to the other inmates. My standing improved. The prison's kingpins then got closer to me. It was really special for a nineteen-year-old to have the support of prison leaders."

Quesnel was soon inducted into a world of violence and terror. He started to snort PCP every day. An industrial quantity of the drug was moving freely through the prison. It was the most common drug available at the time. Hash and cocaine were available as well. PCP wreaks havoc among inmates, often causing users to hallucinate. Many go completely around the bend. The extremely strange drug-induced behaviour of some inmates, on top of clan wars inside the prison, created a highly explosive atmosphere. A man could be killed just for giving someone a funny look.

"By now I was hanging around with the gang that ran the pen. Let's just say, no one bothered us. We controlled everything, and most guards were afraid of us. We were rarely in a normal condition, which probably worried them. We were always plotting something. One day, I'd decided to give a lesson to another inmate, a rapist called Mike. The guy was six-foot-four and weighed two hundred and fifty pounds. I mentioned my plan to Martin, another friend of mine. We went to the prison yard, where Mike was jogging. I had an iron bar. Martin and I were walking along the track while the other fellow was jogging. I told Martin, 'Tell me when he draws level to us.' When I got the signal, I turned around and hit the guy with all my strength right in the face. He started backing up, then fell to his knees. I wanted to go up to him to finish the job, but Martin stopped me, thinking the guards might see us. I tossed the iron bar in the yard and the inmate managed to stand up. He staggered back inside while Martin and I continued to walk in the yard."

Incidents like this happened frequently. The other inmates learned to fear Quesnel, who already had a reputation for being underhanded and for attacking anyone. This made him the perfect soldier for many of the kingpins who often called on his services. Quesnel loathed all forms of authority and had decided to make a mark in his own way. No one could reason with him any longer.

One day, his father visited him and when he realized the state of mind his son was in, he began to cry. Quesnel was upset to see his father weeping in front of the other inmates and asked his father not to visit him again. Quesnel's father left Donnacona heartbroken, recognizing his son was beyond redemption.

He says, "I cried for an hour and a half. I was unable to see my son in that place. I was completely lost. We didn't speak or see each other for five years. I felt that I'd failed, and I questioned myself. Often. I had to let go. There was nothing else I could do."

The arrival of another young criminal at Donnacona didn't help Quesnel improve in the least. The guy was bold. An outstanding fighter who didn't know the meaning of the word *pity*, whenever he attacked someone it was with the intention of seriously injuring or killing him. The man was called Nose, because his was large.

"Nose came to speak to me as soon as he arrived. We'd met previously at Orsainville. Nose saw who I was hanging around with. We quickly became friends, and a mutual trust was established between us. I wanted him at my side, since he was a really tough guy. Nose was withdrawn and didn't speak much. But he was a great fighter. It was obvious he'd learned to use his fists at a very young age. We quickly became inseparable."

The duo was explosive and feared by most inmates. They were quickly drafted by the prison's tough guys, as though they were talented young hockey players. Taken under the wing of career criminals, Quesnel and Nose were thrust into the major leagues of crime. Prison authorities considered Plamondon, Péruta, and company as irredeemable, so how did two nineteen-year-olds doing their first prison terms end up with these heavyweights?

According to Insp. Pierre Frenette, Quesnel didn't need anyone to influence him. "The authorities decided to send Quesnel to Donnacona at age nineteen, because his case was serious. Given his behaviour, it was the only place to put him. I don't think he needed anyone to tell him what to do. Look at his history. Quesnel worked very hard to earn a reputation for being tough and merciless. Let's not forget that his goal was to become a really big shot, and that he did everything needed to reach it. This was the quickest way to reach his goal. He had rejected all social values and followed his plan very carefully, wanting to catch the attention of major criminal organizations. He wanted to be drafted."

"Nose and I had cells in the same prison wing, and had taken control of it," Quesnel says. "We drank quite a bit and stirred things up. There was always PCP around and music, usually loud. It was rather crazy. The girl-friend of one of the bigwigs in our group managed to get a lot of dope brought in. A buddy of mine on the outside, with links to the Quebec City Hells Angels, would send me money. It was simple: this guy wanted me with him after my release and he took care of me. I lived in grand style while in jail and wanted for nothing. We were all crazy and always stoned. The guards were afraid of us. Sometimes, just to be annoying, I'd spit in front of them, and they'd just lower their eyes."

"There was a lot of tension at Donnacona peniten-tiary," says Stéphane, a former guard who worked there between 1990 and 1994. "I left that world because I was at the end of my rope, and wouldn't work there again, even if I were starving. I was ready to kill an inmate. They rankled us all the time and had even threatened to kill my children. Inmates often have nothing to lose. Some of them are locked up forever. I remember Quesnel. He loved to mouth off in front of other inmates and was always trying to outsmart someone. When we were alone with him, however, he spoke decently. It wasn't an easy place to work in. There were a lot of drugs around. It was hell."

Violence, intimidation, and threats were part of Quesnel's everyday life. His group was feared. In the evenings, only Quesnel and his friends stayed out of their cells; the other inmates took refuge inside theirs.

"At Donnacona, few inmates go out after sunset. It's usually the time for settling scores and so most guys are afraid to leave their cells. Only a few of us would stay in the yard or gym. We did as we pleased, snorting, drinking, and smoking joints in front of the guards. They didn't say a word. Other inmates always let us win when we played pool with them. One night, I got drunk on prison-made alcohol – it tasted like rubbing alcohol – and fell on the ice outside. I split my head open and was taken to the infirmary on a stretcher. I was so drunk that I threw up on the nurse."

Quesnel was feared to the point that prison authorities no longer wanted to give him any work. At first, he was assigned to the sports crew, but quickly lost his job. He and the other inmates responsible for the snow blowers were caught stealing gasoline, planning to use it to make Molotov cocktails. Quesnel went to the prison school for a while, but it didn't last. He spent more time thinking about sleeping or drugging the instructor than about the coursework.

"The teacher was in her fifties. We didn't like her because she always insisted that we listen and wouldn't let us sleep in class. One day, Fat Mimi, a member of Montreal's Gang de l'Est, got the idea of putting LSD into her coffee. We slipped two hits into it, and I think she suspected something. I purposely went up to her to ask a question, something I usually never did. As she was answering, I moved my pencil from left to right before her eyes. At one point, I noticed that the acid was taking effect. She started to laugh. At break time, she grabbed her jacket and quickly left the classroom. She was immediately taken to hospital."

Quesnel would see this woman again a few years later in front of the Gabrielle-Roy Library in Quebec City. Visibly afraid, she greeted him before quickly slipping away.

Another Donnacona teacher got a taste of the prisoners' medicine. One of her students – the top student, no doubt – dropped a few Polident tablets, the oxygenated salts used to clean dentures, into the aquarium.

"The water became blue and began to bubble. The teacher was crying. The fish were trying to eat the bubbles, but it didn't last long. They died a few seconds later. The guys thought this was very funny. After that, I stopped going to school and instead did as I pleased, spending my days horsing around in the common room. I'd get up late, around 11 A.M., and would join my friends after lunch. At the time, I was often sent to the hole, an isolated area where they let you out only for an hour a day, and never at the same time as the other prisoners. However, the guys from the inmate committee came to see me, to make sure everything was fine, bringing me drugs as well. I spent my days watching TV completely stoned."

The only visitor Quesnel had was his mother, who came to see him regularly. It was during one of those visits that Quesnel first saw Chantal, Nose's sister. The young blonde caught everyone's eye, and Quesnel was immediately smitten with her. But this infatuation didn't temper his criminal ambitions in the least, and he continued his escapades inside the prison.

"In September 1992, there was a mini-riot in the prison yard. The guards had found a 9 mm pistol, two magazines containing twenty-three bullets, and money inside a log that was to be used to make a campfire. Eight prisoners, including members of the inmate committee, with Colosse in the lead, were sent to the hole. The other inmates were saying the guards had set us up to undermine our group. So about 160 prisoners refused to return to their cells at the end of the evening. They started setting fires all over the yard, using picnic tables and strips from the edge of the skating rink. They also set fire to a hundred-foot-tall light tower. Firemen came and sprayed everything through the fences.

"That night, I took advantage of the riot to try to murder a guy named Jacques Dupras. Fat Mimi, the guy with the Gang de l'Est, had offered me $10,000 to kill him. I'd mentioned this to Martin, the man who'd helped me knock out the rapist, offering him $5,000 to help me again. When the riot broke out, we each had an iron bar and were watching Dupras, who was standing near the rink. He kept looking around and seemed to suspect something, so we couldn't get close to him. We had to be careful, because Dupras was big and strong. At one point, because of the fire, all the lights went out in the yard. We told ourselves it was the time to get him. As we were about to attack, the lights came back on. The guards had set up a generator. So we dropped our plan."

Dupras died in his cell a few months later at the age of thirty-three, stabbed no fewer than thirty-five times with a homemade "spike," an eight-inch nail with a taped handle that's often used to settle scores in prison. The nail was driven straight through his heart. Two brothers, Luc and Yves-Réal Côté, were charged with the crime.

Quesnel kept up his regime of terror. He wanted to be promoted and was willing to do anything to get noticed. Soon he was asked to kill a guy named Gerry.

"I asked Yvon [another inmate] to help me and he agreed. An Angel had asked me to kill Gerry, who had the nasty habit of bad-mouthing the Hells Angels. The biker who gave me the mission had been in Lennoxville in 1985 during the famous purge, where several bikers were killed by their 'brothers.' Their bodies were put in sleeping bags, then thrown into the river. The Hells Angels offered me money to kill Gerry, but that's not why I wanted to do it; knocking him off would entitle me to drugs and other privileges. Besides, I really liked the Hells Angels. This was a good opportunity to be noticed by the organization. So I accepted the biker's offer.

"My plan was simple. I would offer Gerry my help while he was doing bench presses. I told Yvon, 'On my signal, give him a good punch in the balls.' So we went over to Gerry, who was lying on his back on the bench. I said I'd lift the weight while Yvon sat on his legs to stabilize him. He agreed, and I asked him to move back as far as possible. I wanted his head to extend beyond the bench. My goal was to drop the weight right in his face to break his neck. The plan nearly worked. On my signal, Yvon hit him hard, and I dropped the four-hundred-pound barbell on his head. But Gerry moved his head at the last second, and the weight didn't hit him like I wanted it to. He slipped off the bench and fell to the ground, looking dizzy. Not wanting to give him a chance, I immediately grabbed a weight and hit him again on the head. He still managed to get up and run away. Yvon and I took to our feet before he reached the guards. I was caught and put in the hole – again."

Quesnel regularly ended up in isolation. Yet, even in the hole, he managed to get a few grams of drugs. He knew what was going on in the rest of the prison population.

It is surprising how easily Quesnel managed to fool his victims, even though he was increasingly feared on the inside. In only a few months, he had made it into the rank of the prison's toughest characters. Quesnel always had a "spike" nearby.

Since Quesnel was bold, and since his friend Nose was pretty good with his fists, the most respected inmates often asked the pair to do their dirty work, and Quesnel and Nose would do it. They had a mission; they had decided to prove that they would stop at nothing.

"Shortly after I left the hole, following my episode with Gerry, I was asked to kill Michel 'Coriace' Landry. I didn't know why Landry had to die. I had no problem with him. On the contrary, I thought he was okay. But I took the contract anyway. I thought it was especially easy because Landry and I were in the same wing. A few days later we were playing cribbage in the common room, completely stoned on PCP. We were talking about this and that when, suddenly, he told me he had a sore back. I told him that I knew of a cure, and he was interested.

"Later that afternoon, while we were returning to our cells, I told Landry to get ready, that I had to drop by my cell before dealing with his back. I picked up my spike, then went to join him. Landry had left his large radio in the common room, and I told him to leave it there, because I wanted to take it after I killed him. He refused. When we got to his cell, I asked him to lie down on his stomach with his hands behind his head. I pulled out my weapon, striking powerfully on his back, trying to reach his heart. But I think I got him in the spine. He gave a start, and I immediately hit him again. I heard a muffled sound. I thought I'd pierced one of his lungs. I wanted to be done with it because he was strong. But he managed to get up and grab my hand. In fact, he was so worked up that he bent the spike. I then heard the device that automatically closes cell doors and hurried off to my cell. The guards counted the inmates and, a few minutes later, the doors reopened. Wondering what was happening with Landry, I stuck my head out of my cell, looking toward his. Suddenly, he poked his head out as well and looked me in the eyes.

" 'What got into you?'

" 'I don't know.'

" 'Why did you do that to me?'

" 'No idea. A bad trip, but it's over now. Let's go eat supper.'

"We went to get trays and headed for the common room. Landry again asked me why I'd stabbed him. I gave him the same answer. But he then started asking everyone why I'd spiked him. Everyone knew about it, and I was afraid of being caught and sent to the hole. That night, I called my friends together in the gym, telling them what had happened and asking Nose to help me kill Landry. We even asked one of Landry's friends, Luc, to give us a hand. In fact, we gave him no choice. Either he helped us or we'd beat him up. Luc's job was to lure Landry into a dark corner of the gym where Nose and I would be waiting for him. Luc tried many times, but Landry wouldn't play along, he was very suspicious and trusted no one. A little later on, when he saw me with some of my friends, Landry came over. He told Colosse what had happened, and asked him why I had stabbed him. Colosse answered that he wasn't aware of the incident. Then, to make fun of Landry, Colosse started bawling me out, saying I should leave the 'little guy' alone. I promised I wouldn't do it again. Landry waited a few days before going to the infirmary. I kept telling him to go and see the nurse. I was afraid he'd die because everyone knew I stabbed him. The guards and inmates talked to each other a lot. In the end, although Landry had bled internally, he made a full recovery."

He recovered well enough, anyhow, to sue Quesnel nearly three years after the incident. On the advice of a well-known criminal lawyer, Landry sued Quesnel for $200,000, knowing full well that Quesnel had just signed a lucrative deal with the Quebec government for becoming an informant.

Meanwhile, the violence continued at Donnacona. Quesnel, Nose, and another inmate were next asked to kill a prisoner named Claude. Their plan was to lure him to a dark corner of the gym where the three accomplices would attack him with spikes.

"I went to see Claude to offer him cocaine and he asked me to sell him some. I told him to follow me. The inmate helping Nose and me went to get a knife he'd made with a skate blade. When we got to the dark corner, while I pretended to be looking for something in my pockets, our accomplice walked up behind Claude. He was wearing a scarf over his face and we could only see his eyes. I don't know why, but he froze. Nose and I were wondering what was happening. Then Claude finally saw the guy behind him and ran away. I was staggered, and asked the guy why he didn't follow through. He told me that he didn't have time."

In 1999, this accomplice was sentenced to life in prison with the possibility of parole in 2011. While at Donnacona, he phoned a QPF officer and confessed that he'd killed another prisoner nine years earlier. He said that the inmates who controlled the prison had given him a spike and ordered him to kill André "Printemps" Talbot, leader of the Pacific Rebels biker gang. While playing cards in the prison yard, Talbot was stabbed in the back just once, but once was enough. Even if a prison camera had filmed the scene, authorities wouldn't have been able to identify Talbot's killer as the murder took place in a crowd of fifty-two prisoners. The killer got away with it until 1999, when he decided to confess. It had become too much for him to bear over the years. A few months following Talbot's murder, his killer was himself stabbed twenty-two times with a spike but managed to survive.

"That's how scores are settled in prison. The method is as old as the hills, but it has proven itself. The law of the strongest prevails. Today, I'm angry at the individuals who asked me to commit those crimes. They probably wanted me to be caught so that I would spend my life behind bars with them and ensure their protection. I was a little naive. Those guys will probably never leave jail and they need young people who aren't afraid."

When the inmate was stabbed twenty-two times, it wasn't the first time that someone had tried to kill him. Quesnel himself took part in two of those earlier attempts. All the prisoners knew that this man took all kinds of drugs, and that's what Quesnel used to try to kill him.

"I was asked to kill him and decided to do so during midnight mass. My 'target' was the verger. I asked Mimi, the guy from the Gang de l'Est, to get me a gram of pure PCP, which is equivalent to thirty grams on the street. The night of the mass, while we were all in the chapel, I slipped the drug into a cup of coffee. I offered it to the verger and he took it. I asked him if he wanted me to put a little PCP in it and he said yes. So I added more and was absolutely sure he'd die. As he drank the coffee, his attitude gradually changed. He grew stiff, with tight arms and a wide-eyed stare. As verger, he held the chalice in which we dipped our host. We lined up while he stood straight as a rail. He liked to think he was the priest. It was funny. As the service went on, I told myself, he's going to fall, it's a sure bet. But he kept standing, though he was completely stoned. Once the service was over, I asked another inmate to take him to his cell. I didn't want the guards to see him in that condition. I thought he would die in his sleep, but he didn't. Someone told me later that the verger had moaned all night and that the guards had taken him to the infirmary. It took him ten days to come down, and all that time, I was sure he'd die. He had the reputation of getting stoned on anything, and he lived up to it. I never thought he'd survive such a huge dose of PCP."

About three months later, Quesnel and Nose were once again given the mission of setting a trap for the same inmate. This time, they didn't have to do much. Their job was to lure him into a dark corner of the gym offering him drugs. Once there, another prisoner would stab him.

"The plan was simple. It consisted of taking advantage of the guy's weakness for drugs. He'd consume anything. So I went up to him near the weights and offered him Valium. I had ten pills. He told me, 'I'll take five right away and keep the others for later.' I answered that he could forget my offer if he didn't take all of them at once. So he swallowed all the pills. And I then offered him cocaine and heroin, which came from the group that wanted to kill him. Nose was with me. I was spreading heavy lines of coke, which the guy sniffed, and smaller ones for my partner and me. The guy was so impressed with the drugs that he no longer suspected a thing. And then the killer showed up, discreetly, holding a knife that was about eighteen inches long made out of a hinge taken from the outdoor skating rink. Our guy was stabbed in the back while snorting. He turned around, but Nose and I grabbed his arms. While struggling, he was stabbed in the face, but he managed to break free and run away. Nose and the guy with the knife also left quickly. A guard fired a warning shot, and I remained in the corner of the gym for a while, not wanting to be seen by the guards. Before heading to my cell, I took off a few garments, which I gave to another inmate in the gym, who got rid of them. I wasn't caught, and the victim respected the law of the place by keeping his mouth shut."

Such attacks were on the increase during Quesnel's prison term. He was continually mixed up in settling scores. People used him, although he didn't realize it at the time, as he was much too busy trying to make a name for himself. Quesnel modelled his behaviour on that of the characters he hung around with in jail. He took all kinds of drugs. He also frequently visited the prison's tattooer, getting his arms covered with twenty or so drawings.

Quesnel's mother, who visited him every two weeks, couldn't help but see that her son was up to his neck in crime and violence. She was unable to reason with him. No one could. At that point in his life – his early twenties – Quesnel was proud of being among the most feared and despicable group of inmates. His disciplinary file grew continually. He was cited for resisting all form of legal authority, consuming drugs and alcohol, beating and trying to kill prisoners, trafficking drugs, threatening staff, possessing weapons, in short, for living life his own way.

"Cell doors opened automatically at 8 A.M. Most inmates would get up then and go for breakfast, but I stayed in bed since I didn't work. I'd even warned other inmates not to drag their feet on the floor since that woke me up. One day, Nose slashed a prisoner's face with an X-acto knife for that reason. We often slept till lunch. Then, while other prisoners went to work, we spent the afternoon playing cards, talking, watching TV, and especially getting stoned in the common room. We'd smoke joints and snort drugs in front of the guards, who didn't say a word because we intimidated them. They didn't dare do a thing."

Quesnel and his friends used the same treatment – intimidation – on other inmates. They got everything they wanted merely by asking. By now, most inmates were afraid of this man who had made a name for himself so quickly.

"One day while I was in the gym, I asked Stéphane Malouin to wave at another inmate to come to join us. As soon as he stepped through the doorway, we hit the guy hard in the face with a baseball bat. We knocked him out just for kicks. The worst thing is that Malouin got the rap. I thought it was really funny."

Stéphane Malouin made headlines in December 1994 after being murdered with a spike. He was attacked in the gym in front of some sixty inmates. Twenty-eight years old, Malouin was playing pool when he was attacked by another prisoner. He was stabbed all over his body and his carotid artery was severed. Stéphane Sills was sentenced for that crime in 1997. This wasn't the first time Malouin had been attacked. He'd been stabbed a few times with a spike in February of the same year and had to be hospitalized. It's believed he'd fallen afoul of the Gang de l'Est and the Pelletier brothers. That year, 1994, was a particularly bloody one at the Donnacona jail. No fewer than forty-six violent incidents were registered, twelve of them requiring the hospitalization of inmates.

"Sometimes, with all the drugs we took, our minds played tricks on us," Quesnel says. "I remember one night, when Nose and I were in the Donnacona gym, really stoned on PCP, I thought some of the other inmates were staring at me. I panicked, and ran off and pulled out a huge metal post that held the badminton net. I was running around with the post and screaming. Nose, who was as stoned as I was, took a pool cue and broke it in half. He then began spinning the pieces as though he were Bruce Lee. We were totally delirious, and the other inmates were starting to worry. Nose even took off his shirt in front of an old prisoner who looked like he was about to have a heart attack. At that point, Louis, one of the inmates, approached to calm us down, saying that everything was fine and no one wanted to hurt us. Afterwards, people talked about this incident for some time."

Drugs make up a huge part of prisoners' lives. It's their way of escaping prison. When Quesnel was at Donnacona, several dozen prisoners took PCP daily. It's no wonder that completely crazy incidents occurred.

"Sometimes prisoners did very zany things. One day, Claude, the inmate I tried to kill, surprised everyone by standing on the bench press reserved for the Hells Angels. He stripped completely and started shouting incomprehensible words. This could've caused many problems for him. Another time, during an AA meeting, an inmate who was really stoned 'distinguished' himself. The prisoner, a native, had made a cake for a guy celebrating the twentieth anniversary of his being sober. But the native guy, like us, had snorted a few lines of PCP. During the meeting, he started walking and clucking like a chicken. We were all dying of laughter. He made his way to the front of the room and began stuffing his face with cake, using his hands, repeatedly asking if it was good. The AA people got so scared that they left, never to return."

At one point Quesnel managed to get sixteen grams of PCP smuggled into the jail. Michel "Pit" Caron was behind this special delivery.

"I'd tried to cut the drug, but it was still really powerful. At night, in my cell, I could hear inmates who'd taken it throwing up. It was awful. The next day, in the gym, guys linked to the Rock Machine came to see me. They were convinced I'd tried to kill them. Following a few explanations, they changed their minds. I could've had problems with that drug."

Quesnel learned a great deal during his time in prison. Not that he took advantage of his stay to do some thinking and mend his ways. Quite the opposite. The penitentiary allowed Quesnel to mix with the fiercest criminals and to realize he had all the tools needed to succeed in their world. At least, that was what he thought at the time. All those around him valued crime. The toughest individuals were those who were most respected, and Quesnel wanted to be respected. In 1991 he was finally released, and immediately took up with his old friends.

"Naturally, I quickly took up with the underworld again. Since I had to earn a living and had no intention of working, I went back to stealing."

He decided to rob the Royal Bank in Quebec City's Limoilou neighbourhood at gunpoint and plotted the heist with his friend Pat.

"We wore caps and sunglasses. Since I didn't want to take any risks, I disguised the tattoos on my face. We were armed. A friend of mine who was linked to the Quebec City Hells Angels had lent me a .38, and Pat had borrowed a .38 from his brother. We entered the bank and Pat shouted, 'This is a holdup!' I then ran to jump over the counter, but my feet caught on the edge and I fell to the ground beside a teller who started to scream. I put my revolver to her head, and ordered her to be quiet. Her till was open. I took all the money in it, then ran up to Pat. We fled on our bikes. After ditching them behind a government building, we continued on foot, taking refuge at Pat's sister's place, in an apartment building. We counted the money, splitting up about $1,000. We stashed the weapons, and I left in a taxi. Later that evening, I gave the .38 back to its owner. Everything went well."

Quesnel also sold drugs for a man linked to the Quebec City Hells Angels. For a time, he was dealing about four ounces of cocaine and PCP a week. Although lucrative, this job didn't last long. Quesnel was arrested after carrying out an armed robbery in a caisse populaire in Saint-Émile, north of Quebec City. He was sentenced to three years and sent back to Donnacona penitentiary, picking up where he'd left off: drugs, fights, conspiracies, attempted murders, and everything that goes along with them.

In the summer of 1993, Quesnel was released, and Nose followed him out a few months later. That fall, the two tough guys killed Richard Jobin and Martin Naud before being arrested over a fight, and again went back to Donnacona.

"I'd returned to the fold. My reputation was established. Certain organizations were starting to take an interest in Nose and me. We were always together, and had proved we could do whatever we were asked to. We were starting to think about which organization we'd prefer to work with, and often talked about it. The Montreal mafia were looking our way through the agency of some of its members who were imprisoned with us. Same thing for Montreal's Gang de l'Est and the Pelletier brothers. Nose let me decide for the two of us since I'd be the first released. At one point, when we were allowed to receive guests in the gym, Fat Mimi introduced me to his boss, Sylvain 'le Blond' Pelletier, leader of the Gang de l'Est. He was with his brother and Claude 'le Pic' Rivard, whom I would murder a few years later. Pelletier was rich, and the network he managed was suspected of several crimes. Our meeting was brief, since visitors were waiting for us. Pelletier asked me to contact him on my release from prison. Back then, I thought that leaving Quebec City was an interesting idea. Montreal is much larger and I thought I could more easily blend into the crowd there."

In the summer of 1994, Quesnel was again released after saying farewell to his pals. He was convinced that his path through the world of crime was set, and felt wanted. Among his contacts were some of the province's most important criminals. But he also felt the need to enjoy life a little.

"When I left prison, I didn't need money, since I could already count on a couple of thousand dollars my clients owed me. As I was under close surveillance and required to visit the police and my probation officer every week, I decided to take it easy. I wanted to have a good time and get closer to Chantal, Nose's sister. We'd had a relationship since the previous fall, and I loved her. However, investigators suspected me of wanting to kill a cop. The police were targeting me, but this didn't prevent my meeting le Blond Pelletier in a Quebec City restaurant. He officially asked me to join his group, explaining he had problems with the Hells Angels, who had dealers in places he controlled. Pelletier was determined not to be pushed around and asked me to become a killer for the Gang de l'Est. This would earn me between $10,000 and $20,000 a murder, plus $500 a week. I was interested. I asked him to give me a few days, enough time to finish my probation."

Quesnel was fully aware that the situation between the Pelletier clan and the Hells Angels was likely to deteriorate. He was aware of the bikers' reputation and knew they wouldn't back down. But Pelletier's offer was tempting. It was the kind of work he was looking for. He told his friends that he had decided to leave Quebec City for Montreal.

"I mentioned this to Pit Caron, who thought the idea very good. I wanted to drop out of sight so I wouldn't have to advise the authorities about my change of address. I had a few days to spare. But a phone call from my probation officer radically changed my plans."

The probation officer asked him to come to his office. He had a surprise in store for Quesnel.

"When I reached his office, the probation officer read me a directive from Correctional Services. He wanted a urine sample, so that he could have it analyzed to make sure I wasn't taking drugs or alcohol, one of the conditions of my release. I carefully read the regulation, and told him I didn't need to urinate at that moment. So he asked me to come back a few hours later. As soon as I left the office, I rushed to the drugstore to buy a substance used to flush out kidneys. Then I went to a gym to buy a product used for colouring urine. When I got back home, I drank a huge amount of those two products, as well as lots of water. I wanted to eliminate as much of the compromising residue as possible before returning to see the officer. I was crossing my fingers."

Quesnel realized that his freedom hung by a thread. He tried to dismiss gloomy ideas as best he could, but he felt hounded.

"Two days after the urine test, while I was at my friend Sandra Beaulieu's place, the doorbell rang. It was the RCMP. They knew I was there and told Sandra they had a warrant. They asked me to go with them, and I did. During the drive back to Donnacona, I was seething with anger and frustration, but I didn't say a word. However – and that's what helped me deal with what was happening – I knew I'd only spend a few days in jail. Just long enough to complete my last sentence."

Quesnel's return to prison didn't faze him. Donnacona was in many ways his territory. His friend Nose greeted him with open arms.

"Nose was happy to see me. I told him I'd decided to join le Blond's clan. Since he was going to follow me, he was happy as well. We'd found our employer. Deep down, I wanted to be with the Hells Angels, but they were very selective. The Donnacona inmates who belonged to Pelletier's group were very happy that Nose and I had decided to join them. All we had to do was await our release, and mine was quickly approaching."

Once again, however, an unexpected visit changed the course of events. Quesnel's lawyer came to the penitentiary to see some of his clients, among them the soon-to-be-released Quesnel.

"He wanted to say hi and ask what I planned to do when I got out. So I took advantage of the situation, knowing that he represented several members of the Hells Angels. I trusted him. So I decided to tell him all about the Pelletier clan's offer, writing some things down in case the jail's small meeting room was bugged. I wanted to send the Angels a message: they were going to lose a good soldier. I told the lawyer everything. He was very attentive, and even took notes. Before leaving, he promised he'd come back to see me before my release. I knew he'd call his clients. I told Nose everything, warning him not to repeat a word. If they'd found out, our friends at the time could have suddenly become our enemies. Had Pelletier learned I was in touch with the Angels, he would've had me killed. He was very popular at Donnacona. He'd give small gifts to the big shots, and had the power to kill anyone behind bars."

A few days later, the lawyer returned to Donnacona and asked to see Quesnel. The two were brought to a small windowed office watched over by guards.

"Again, we communicated in hushed voices and in writing. We couldn't take any risks. At times, he'd whisper into my ear, which perplexed the guard, Alain Giguère, who was looking at us with a slight smile that said a lot. The meeting was brief. The lawyer told me that a biker wanted to see me on my release. I knew it was the Hells Angels, and asked him whether it was the Quebec City chapter. He said it wasn't. He told me to call him as soon as I got out and to keep our conversation secret."

Quesnel was euphoric as he left the room, and he immediately went to tell Nose.

"The door was now wide open for us to join the most prestigious biker gang in the world. The bikers were the ones who wanted us. We were in a position of strength. I thought this was the opportunity of a lifetime. From then on, nothing could change my destiny. I was ready to do anything to climb to the top of the organization. I wanted to become a millionaire."

A few days before Quesnel left Donnacona, Sylvain "le Blond" Pelletier was killed in a bomb explosion. Quesnel conveyed his sympathies to Fat Mimi.

"Mimi asked me to join the organization anyhow, and even gave me a phone number to call on my release.

I was anxious to leave Donnacona and increasingly tired of putting on an act. I'd even said I wanted to avenge Pelletier's death. With the hatred that this murder elicited among Donnacona inmates, it was in my interest to say nothing about my plans. I felt a little bad about being a traitor, but had no choice. I knew that my prison friends would become my enemies as soon as I joined the Hells Angels. They belonged to the rival organization, and I was to become an Angel. The only thing I still had to do was to meet my employer."

Quesnel was released in early November 1994 and went back to Chantal's. The couple was happy to be reunited. As he'd agreed, Quesnel contacted his lawyer, who arranged to see him at the Quebec City courthouse.

"We were to meet in front of Room 2.22 inside the courthouse. On the way, I wondered about many things and was very anxious to know the identity of my future employer. I spotted my lawyer as I arrived in front of Room 2.22. There were many detectives waiting to testify. Some of their faces were familiar. The lawyer asked me to follow him into the bathroom so we could chat discreetly. He told me to meet him at his house that night."

Quesnel took advantage of the few spare hours he had to visit his friend Michel "Pit" Caron in Beauport. The two men talked about life in general and Quesnel borrowed clothes from his friend. He then went back to Chantal's.

"Finally, night fell and I headed to my lawyer's place. He lived in a prestigious house opposite the Plains of Abraham, in the same neighbourhood as Premier Jacques Parizeau. His office took up part of the first floor and could be accessed from a door on the side of the house. Inside the entrance was a large hallway, and on the walls were several laminated newspaper articles concerning cases he had won. He greeted me with a handshake and asked that I follow him to his office.

"'Do you know Melou?' he asked.

"'No,' I answered.

"'He's an Angel from Trois-Rivières and he'd like to meet you. My associate will drive you to him.'

"'Where's the meeting?'

"'In a Montreal restaurant.'

"'I'd prefer to meet him at the Trois-Rivières club-house.'

"'Wait. I'll make a phone call.'

"The lawyer grabbed the phone and called the famous Melou. He told him, 'I've got your guy in front of me. He'd prefer meeting you at the clubhouse. Does that suit you? Okay. Goodbye.'

"'It's settled. You'll go to the Trois-Rivières club-house Friday. Melou will be there.'

"'Thanks.'

"'Remember what I'm about to tell you. I put the two of you in touch and that's all. I'm not responsible for how Melou acts toward you, and I told Melou the same thing.'

"I was wondering about certain things when I left. Who was this Melou? Why Trois-Rivières, a town smaller than Quebec City? I was very anxious to get the answers."

3

THE DREAM

WE ALL HAVE DREAMS, and Serge Quesnel's came true on November 4, 1994. He'd been out of Donnacona penitentiary barely three days when he was invited to the Hells Angels' clubhouse in Trois-Rivières.

Melou was the nickname of Louis Roy, president of the chapter and, at the time, a man widely considered to be the most powerful Angel in Quebec. He was certainly one of the richest. Although he tried to stay out of the news, he was often mentioned in the media. He was born in the Saguenay region, and everyone there knew who he was, many of them considering him to be a celebrity. The various police forces watching him at the time were unable to nab him. Even the tax man was after him, since the earnings he was declaring didn't match his standard of living.

Quesnel knew the man he was about to meet only by reputation. But Quesnel was in seventh heaven and raring to go. In his view, the Angels were the top. They were the university of crime. He was sure that he had already passed all the introductory courses, and fully intended to demonstrate this.

On November 4, Quesnel arrived at the majestic biker clubhouse on Highway 55 in Trois-Rivières-Ouest. The building looked like a castle, was bombproof and surrounded by a six-foot wooden palisade. A sign in front of it warned: Enter at Your Own Risk. Quesnel stopped his car in front of the gate and rolled down the window to talk to an invisible biker through the inter-com. He knew he was being watched from the inside through a camera.

"A voice asked what I wanted, and I said, 'I'm here to see Melou.' The gate opened and the way was clear. My first observation was that the yard was very well laid out. To my right was a large white garage with several red doors, painted in the colours of the Hells Angels. What immediately drew my attention was the lit sign on the garage. It featured the winged head of the Hells Angels against a white backdrop with red letters to identify the Trois-Rivières chapter. I was very impressed. Whether you like it or not, the Angels' emblem is striking. I also noticed the in-ground pool and the exterior bar, just like in the south. I didn't know much about the Trois-Rivières bikers, thinking they were a small and rather quiet group. I'd soon discover that it was the most violent chapter in the country. After climbing out of my car, I noticed two guys inside the clubhouse watching me from a window. I walked by a luxurious mauve Mercedes 500 SL convertible parked right in front of the club-house door. Someone opened the bulletproof door and I walked in. I wasn't nervous. Somewhat excited, certainly, but not nervous.

"Two men were waiting for me. The first to hold out his hand had a very young face. He was Louis 'Melou' Roy. He looked like he was in charge of things. I knew he was president of the Trois-Rivières chapter, as well as an experienced businessman. In fact, the Mercedes parked in the entrance belonged to him. At first glance, I was a little surprised, since he wasn't as I imagined him. We looked each other in the eyes, and I held his gaze. We immediately clicked. He introduced me to the man beside him, Frenchy, a prospect for the group. Prospects generally do all the tasks that bikers give them, because they want to become full-patch members of the club, the ones who give orders. Prospects are usually the most dangerous of those who hang around with the Angels. When I met Frenchy, I was stunned by his cold eyes. He was wearing a coat and kept his hands in his pockets. I knew he was holding a gun and that he was ready to use it. The bikers didn't know me then, and the Angels are notorious for being wary. I knew that I was entering the major leagues of crime and that things were getting pretty serious. My criminal career was taking off. I wanted two things: to make money and to get my colours, to be a Hells Angel. Even if the bikers were right to be suspicious of a newcomer like me, they must have trusted the lawyer who'd sent me. After all, he was also Melou's lawyer."

Once inside the clubhouse, Quesnel looked around, trying to register the important details, noticing the pool table, the large gaming room with the pinball machine and the impressive stereo. Melou invited him downstairs and, in accordance with biker tradition, his bodyguard, Frenchy, followed behind to keep an eye on the guest. Quesnel was feeling good. He relaxed, convinced that the chemistry between Melou and him was good. Once downstairs in the meeting room, the three men sat around a large black table. Frenchy kept his hands under the table. Quesnel knew that a revolver was pointed at him. One wrong move would have earned him a few bullets. But the atmosphere was good.

"We started talking about crime and the underworld. Melou asked me what I wanted to do, and I said that I wanted to help them. Melou knew that I'd already killed. We talked about certain Donnacona inmates he'd have liked to see disappear, then, at one point, without warning, he moved on to serious things, asking me to become a killer for the organization. He said, 'Each murder will earn you $10,000 to $25,000. Moreover, you'll be paid $500 a week, and we'll put you up. You'll have to accompany me during the week. I often have to go to Montreal.' He wanted me as his bodyguard, and I understood what he expected of me. I'd get weekends off, and would be able to see my girlfriend in Quebec City. Then, during the conversation, I had a sudden thought and asked whether the room could be bugged. I noticed that, unlike the Quebec City Angels, people here weren't afraid of speaking loudly. Melou began to laugh, telling me, 'This place has never been raided! If there were any bugs in here, I'd have been in jail long ago.' He was very sure of himself. He told me I was making a good decision by joining his group and that I'd help them 'clean up.'"

Quesnel immediately accepted the Hells Angels' offer. The salary mattered little to him, since all he cared about was the chance to prove himself. He wanted the other bikers in the group to accept him as part of the team as quickly as possible, and liked the challenge awaiting him. He felt highly qualified for the "position." He knew he had just signed a pact with Melou, a lifelong pact.

Louis Roy came to Quebec's Mauricie region at the end of the 1980s. He had just made a name for himself among the Angels – and the police – by taking control of the Saguenay-Lac-Saint-Jean territory by eliminating the rival Conquatcheros. Having won a major war, the Missiles, his group in the Saguenay, deserved to establish itself in the Mauricie, with the blessing of the powerful Hells Angels. The site chosen for the new clubhouse was strategically located near all the main roads. Roy soon attracted everyone's attention by building himself a magnificent house valued at $315,000 on Cherbourg Street in Trois-Rivières-Ouest.

On June 23, 1991, the Missiles buried their colours and became the fourth Hells Angels chapter in Quebec. The Trois-Rivières Angels wasted no time in gaining a reputation for violence. During its first year, twenty-four underworld murders were committed, as though by coincidence, murders that were attributed to the new "Reds." An entire chapter of the Outlaws, sworn enemies of the Angels, was wiped out in Joliette. There was much bloodshed. The local population was worried and many people who lived near the clubhouse tried to sell their houses. So did residents on Cherbourg Street, where Louis Roy and a few full-patch members now lived. The mayor of Trois-Rivières-Ouest, Jean-Charles Charest, tried to reassure the public by promising that the police were up to the task. There was a great deal of talk in the community about the new Angels. Journalists who knocked at the clubhouse door were turned away. The same thing happened at Melou's house, where his spouse, Rosalba, politely but firmly told journalists who had the nerve to show up that he had nothing to tell them.

On November 4, 1994, Quesnel joined the chapter.

"Melou asked Frenchy to go upstairs and get $2,000 from the safe. He told me I'd have plenty of work. He was really playing it up, saying I'd even get my own Harley and go riding with the group. He added, 'When the war [with the Rock Machine] is over, you'll stay or go. You'll do as you please.' He was lying, you never leave the Hells Angels. I knew this, but Melou's words didn't bother me. What I wanted was to get money and power quickly, regardless of the means. I also knew I was joining the bikers to stay. It was my dream. I felt lucky to be chosen. Killing for the organization meant that I wouldn't have to do the boring work given to members of affiliated clubs. Anyhow, there was no way I would be a lackey and do the errands that full-patch members didn't want to do. From the beginning I would have a higher status than members of affiliated clubs and could even give orders to them. My years of violence while in jail – my years of service – were being recognized. Melou knew how to win my trust."

When Frenchy came back with the $2,000, Melou handed Quesnel the money, in bills of $50 and $100, telling him to have a really good time over the weekend, to spend all the money. He asked him to return the following Monday and not to buy any clothes. The club would take care of that. The two men said goodbye. As Quesnel drove off, he was happier than he had ever been.

"I was euphoric as I left the place. My head was buzzing with ideas, and the trip from Trois-Rivières to Quebec City seemed very short. However, I had a problem with my car, an old 1985 blue Cougar, and had to have it towed to a garage on Hamel Boulevard. The owner, a friend of mine, had sold me the car. He lent me another, and I went to see my girlfriend. During the weekend with Chantal, all I could think about was my conversation with one of the biggest names in Quebec crime. I was anxious for Monday to come, visualizing my future life as a Hells Angel, as a killer for the Hells Angels. I felt powerful, invincible almost.

"I was happy to be with Chantal again, but when I told her I was moving to Trois-Rivières, alone, she was angry. She resented my accepting the offer without consulting her. I tried to reassure her, saying that the two of us would soon enjoy good times. To win her forgiveness, I used the money Melou gave me to spoil her a little. We went shopping in the Saint-Roch neighbourhood and I bought her a pair of white boots. We decided to spend the weekend at the Maxim Motel. I didn't tell her exactly what I'd be doing for the Hells Angels, and Chantal didn't ask many questions. She was Nose's sister, and members of that family aren't in the habit of making idle talk. We'd been seeing each other for nearly two years at that point, and I thought things between us were serious. Chantal was beautiful. A former dancer, she was a wrestler and able to defend herself. During that weekend, she finally understood that I was now in a good position.

"I also took advantage of the weekend to visit my buddy Pit Caron. I wanted to get his advice. Pit had been close to the Quebec City Hells Angels for a few years. When I told him the news, he said he was happy for me. He knew the Trois-Rivières guys and said I was lucky to be joining them. He also told me that my new 'brothers' were partiers."

After treating himself to a good time over the weekend, Quesnel returned to the Trois-Rivières club-house. He was a little nervous at the idea of meeting new bikers, but calmed his fears by remembering his criminal past, his years in jail, the numerous fights he had had and the ones he started. He thought about his two murders: of Richard Jobin, the garage owner, and Martin Naud. Two murders for which he was never arrested. He had outmanoeuvred the police. Images from the past stood out in his mind, violent images, of badly beaten men, covered in blood, left for dead. Images of corpses.

They made him feel powerful, confident he could face the challenges awaiting him. Quesnel was now in a better frame of mind to meet his new colleagues.

"Frenchy greeted me at the clubhouse. He shook my hand and asked me to follow him to the large room where the bar was located. A few people were there, and Frenchy introduced me to them. I wasn't told anything at the time, but the guys there were all full-patch members. They had a fine bearing, were well dressed, seemed friendly, but didn't talk much. I thought they were studying me, but I pretended not to notice. I felt confident. I took advantage of this second visit to take a good look around. I noticed two large fridges with glass doors containing beer and bottled water, as well as an impressive collection of wine and liquor. In a far corner of the room were photos of all the full-patch members of the various chapters. It was a practical way of identifying strangers. I also saw several sandbags piled up along a wall. I found out a little later that the bags were to be used in case of an attack from the highway. The clubhouse was clean, and everything was in its place. It looked somewhat like a bar."

Melou Roy, Quesnel's boss, was away that day but had left instructions with Frenchy. The new employee of the Trois-Rivières Hells Angels must buy clothes to look a little more civilized and go unnoticed. Roy liked fancy restaurants and large hotels, which meant his men had to be well dressed and have some class. Since cops can't afford expensive restaurants, that's where Roy felt safest.

Frenchy's brother was given the job of going shopping with Quesnel, since Frenchy was working on a contract. Also a killer for the Hells Angels, his mission was to do in a man named Gino Hallé, from Quebec City. According to the Hells Angels court, Hallé was associating a little too much with the Rock Machine, the rival group. This was reason enough to kill him. Frenchy planned the crime with Raven, a full-patch member of the Trois-Rivières chapter who proudly wore the insignia of the Filthy Few, reserved for those who have killed for the organization.

"I was taken to the Laviolette Suites, a hotel located by the Saint-Lawrence River in Trois-Rivières-Ouest. Raven was waiting for me in a room. In a threatening manner, he said he had something to ask me. He wanted to know if I had beaten up his brother-in-law at Donnacona, which I hadn't. Our first conversation didn't last long. Raven also wanted me to have the tears tattooed on my face removed. It would be too easy for a witness to identify me with such a distinctive mark. Raven had a contact in Montreal and wanted to put me in touch with him. He'd started to have a few of his own tattoos removed. After a brief discussion with me, Frenchy and Raven headed for Quebec City. For my part,

I went to buy clothes, which cost the Hells Angels $800, then got a haircut. A few attempts were made to find me an apartment, but to no avail.

"When I got back to the clubhouse, Melou was there and seemed happy to see me. He introduced me to other bikers and took great pains to make me feel good. We went down to the basement and he explained exactly what he expected of me. He told me I'd have plenty of work, that a few people had to be knocked off, and gave me a gun, a Russian-made 9 mm pistol. He also gave me two magazines, each holding seven bullets, and told me that I'd have to ditch all weapons after using them. They could never be traced back to the Angels. He also gave me a pager, so that I could be reached at any time. At this point I told him that I'd rather live in the club-house than in an apartment. So he took me to the second floor to show me a room with a bed, saying, 'This is your room, this is your home.' I was happy. There were two other rooms on the same floor, as well as the observa-tion room. Living there suited me, since I got free room and board. As well, it allowed me to get closer to the other members, who were a little suspicious at first. I felt my every move was being watched, and wanted to show them I was trustworthy."

The observation room in Trois-Rivières contained several TV screens linked to cameras, allowing the biker on guard duty to ensure that everything around the clubhouse was quiet. Each member of the Angels had to take turns doing guard duty every forty-five days. This remains part of biker practice. And it's serious business. The Hells Angels spend a lot of money just to ensure their security. It's in the interest of those on guard duty to take the job seriously. After all, wars cause casualties, and the war with the Rock Machine had begun. Quesnel had to do his turn of duty like the others.

"I had to keep an eye on the screens, which were fitted into a large bookcase. The pictures came from surveillance cameras. One of the cameras was remote-controlled and could be operated from the inside. As well, the six-foot fence enclosing the property around the clubhouse was equipped with motion detectors. An alarm sounded if anyone came too close. When a suspicious vehicle appeared on the street, a description of it had to be entered in the logbook and, when possible, a video recording had to be made using the machine connected to the cameras. The watchman also had to open the gate to visitors after identifying them. When the phone rang, we were always to answer, 'Trois-Rivières,' then transfer the call to the person asked for. Our job was to ensure the security of people who were on Angels property. In case of attack, we were to walk onto the terrace and fire on the aggressors. Everything was ready for that purpose. There were even ramparts on the terrace to give us protection if we were shot at. On a few occasions, I went outside with a rifle when I spotted a suspicious-looking vehicle and, believe me, I wouldn't have hesitated to use it if men had got out of the cars. It was just as well that a few curious individuals didn't stop in front of the clubhouse. I might've opened fire, since war was raging between the gangs and there was no room for mistakes."

Quesnel soon found a way to make the work less monotonous.

"With the camera on the roof, I'd sometimes do a little voyeurism, to pass the time. Using the remote control, I'd point the lens at the windows of nearby houses and try to see something."

From his first days with the Trois-Rivières bikers, Quesnel was impressed. Members lived in grand style, and always seemed to be above everyone else, to be stronger and richer. They liked to put on quite a show with their money. They had it and they flaunted it. This was what impressed newcomers and led them to do anything to become full-patch members. Quesnel saw the bikers gambling at $5,000 a bid. At the end of the evening, some had lost as much as $75,000, but were still smiling. Quesnel couldn't afford to play with them, but he looked on and learned. He also tried to keep up with the gruelling pace of the bikers. Party nights followed one another at a crazy pace and soon began to leave traces on his face.

"After a few weeks of being around the bikers, I was tired. In prison, I was used to a more regular schedule. But at the clubhouse, it was party after party. They were always celebrating. It wasn't unusual for us to turn in at 4 A.M. and get up at 8 A.M. I had trouble adapting. I was losing weight and had circles under my eyes. On those days when we were at the Trois-Rivières clubhouse – it didn't happen too often – I'd take refuge in a rarely occupied basement room to get a little sleep. I was tired but happy, as I had an increasingly important role in the organization's daily operations.

"Melou was the richest Angel in Quebec, and I was his protege. We spent more and more time together, and I was getting to know him. We travelled together, and I could see that he was among the most powerful members of the 'profession.' He carried a booklet with the names, addresses, licence plate numbers, and descriptions of fifty or so undesirable individuals. When I saw it, I realized that the Trois-Rivières Hells Angels were very powerful. I asked Melou when he'd give me 'work,' and he answered that we still had information to gather. The Trois-Rivières bikers controlled a great deal more than their own territory. They did business across the province and controlled several affiliated clubs. Melou introduced me to his friends, all of them very rich. I was getting to know all these wonderful people. Melou seemed to impress a lot of the people around him. Just from the way those who came to shake his hand behaved, I could see he was powerful. When he walked into a place, people got up to greet him.

"Over the first few weeks, the other full-patch members began to trust me. They seemed to value my presence more and more, and often wanted me to accompany them. I realized that, compared to them, I was very poor. I wanted to change that. I was convinced that I would be able to make a lot of money eventually. It was a question of climbing the ladder, one rung at a time. I was anxious to have the chance to impress them and show that I wasn't afraid."

Quesnel struck up a friendship with Richard "Rick" Vallée, another killer for the group. In 1997, Vallée, a member of the Nomads, the Hells Angels' shock troops, was scheduled to appear in a United States court over the murder of an informant for the Drug Enforcement Agency (DEA). The informant, Lee Carter, was blown to pieces in 1993, in Champlain, New York, and explosives were Rick Vallée's specialty. Vallée, who was to be handed over to American authorities, escaped from Saint-Luc Hospital in a manner worthy of a Hollywood movie, giving his two guards the slip. One of Vallée's accomplices was hidden inside the closet of a hospital room, armed with a 12 gauge shotgun, while two others were waiting with motorbikes in front of the building.

Vallée is probably responsible, along with Melou, for merging his former group, the Missiles, with the Angels. He is also suspected of having blown up the vehicle of the president of the Conquatcheros, rivals to the Missiles. Omer Gagnon, alias "Boursoufflé," was twenty-nine years old when he was blown to bits by a homemade bomb in the Saguenay on October 24, 1984. Quesnel remembers Rick Vallée as a cold and hard man.

"Rick said he loved returning to the scene of explosions a few hours afterwards. He liked to see pieces of flesh in trees and on the walls of buildings. I thought he was a little gruesome. He'd say this with a detached expression and an icy gaze. I liked chatting with him. He seemed very human, but appearances were deceiving. We spent time together, and I got to know him better. He seemed to like me, to trust me, and wanted to show me how to use explosives properly. In his view, most people used charges that were too heavy. This meant that the target would be ejected through the vehicle's roof and often managed to survive. Rick said that the trick was to use *only* two sticks of dynamite. That way, the victim remained inside the vehicle and was blown to bits. He led me to understand that he'd blown up le Blond Pelletier and several others."

On October 28, 1994, Sylvain "le Blond" Pelletier, leader of the Montreal clan bearing his name and closely

linked to the Rock Machine, died when his Jeep
Cherokee was destroyed by a bomb in front of his
Repentigny home. His spouse, Kathy Hamond, seven
months pregnant, was coming out of the house when
the blast occurred. Suffering from shock, she had to be
taken to the hospital in an ambulance. The explosion
was so powerful that parts of the vehicle landed many
metres away. Pelletier's body was blown to pieces, and
morgue workers had to use plastic bags to recover his
remains. His name had been on the Hells Angels' black-
list for a long time.

After they got to know each other, Rick Vallée gave
Serge Quesnel a gold ring set with some twenty-four
diamonds. "It was a ring that the Alliance had had made
for each of its members. The Alliance consisted of the
Rock Machine and the Pelletier brothers, and its mission
was to resist the Hells Angels. I quite obviously inher-
ited the ring of an Alliance member killed by the Angels."

Among the other Angels Quesnel hung around
with were Sudiste and Paulo, who were sponsors of the
Blatnois, the Angels' puppet club in Grand-Mère. Luc,
Nachos, and Dan – who would later become president
of the Trois-Rivières Angels – also rubbed shoulders
with Quesnel. Nachos was the person who left a message
on Quesnel's pager, warning him to stay away from the
clubhouse because of a police raid on November 23, 1994.

During the raid, police arrested three of the group's prospects, and seized several high-calibre guns, pistols, and a large amount of ammunition. The Angels were not impressed.

"The day after the raid, Melou told me he'd had a few pizzas sent to the cops who'd searched the place, just to laugh at them. The cops replied by sending him Saint-Hubert chicken, which Melou threw in the garbage."

There was a lot of action in Quesnel's new life and he enjoyed it. During that initial period with the Angels, his car was often pulled over, earning him a fine each time for driving without a licence. He saw his girlfriend in Quebec City once in a while, then left her alone for more or less prolonged intervals. Nachos gave him his first murder contract. The Angels' new recruit was asked to murder Gino Hallé, because the team of killers originally given the job wasn't able to finish it.

"Nachos was offering me $10,000, plus Hallé's hashish run in Quebec City. This suited me. Besides, I knew Hallé and had no objection to killing him. I knew that Nachos supplied part of Quebec City with hashish. He used to be a bartender at the Carol strip club in Quebec City, before he opted for a career change. The new job was more stressful, but more lucrative. He had climbed the ladder and become a full-patch member of the Hells Angels. Nachos didn't like the competition

Gino Hallé was giving him. It was also rumoured that Hallé was telling everyone that the Trois-Rivières Hells Angels had knocked off Sylvain 'le Blond' Pelletier."

So Quesnel headed to Quebec City to meet his friend Pit Caron, who he hoped would help him do the killing. The meeting took place at the Folichon, a strip club on Hamel Street.

"I asked Pit if he wanted to do the contract with me, and offered him $5,000. Pit knew Hallé and agreed. Not only did he know where Hallé lived, he also played hockey with him once a week.

" 'It'll be easy,' I told Pit.

" 'Of course, he's my buddy. I'll call him to schedule a meeting. He'll show up and won't suspect a thing,' Pit said.

"So we celebrated by getting smashed. Next day, we did a reconnaissance mission in a car I'd rented, driving by Hallé's home and the arena where he and Pit played hockey and making our plan in the process. We were very confident. I liked Caron a lot and trusted him, knowing he had good judgment. When I drove him back, I told him to wait till he heard from me, then went to see Chantal."

After a few days' leave, Quesnel returned to the Trois-Rivières clubhouse, where a biker prospect named Mario was waiting for him. Mario told Quesnel that

Melou had planned a major strike and that the two of them had to go to Montreal.

"We drove to Montreal, to the InterContinental Hotel, a very luxurious place where several bikers were waiting for us. There were some twelve of us in a room, including Rick Vallée, Paulo, Ponpon, Damy, Dan, Flat, a biker covered in tattoos, and J.C. Also present were a few prospects and Fat Eddy, president of the Jokers, a Hells Angels puppet club. Frenchy and I were given the job of retrieving all weapons from the various rented vehicles. When we were done, I was impressed with the artillery we'd brought into the room. Then the guys rubbed their fingerprints off their weapons.

"Rick Vallée took charge of the operation and divided everyone into various teams. Each team was given the mission of killing one member of the enemy clan. The atmosphere was good, and I had the impression we were going on a hunting trip. Everyone was relaxed. Melou had got everyone to remove the batteries from their cellphones, since he was afraid that the cops had bugged them. My team was to murder Gilles Lambert, a major player with the Rock Machine. This was serious business. The Hells Angels had decided to strike a major blow by eliminating many of the Rock Machine's bigwigs in Montreal in one go. Rick was offering $50,000 to the team that killed the first rival.

The guys were excited and in a good mood. Suddenly, we heard a noise from outside that sounded like an explosion. Someone asked Rick if this was his doing, but he said that it wasn't. We didn't know what had just exploded. In fact, we didn't even know if it was a bomb, but the guys started making jokes about the Rock Machine being unable to kill anyone with their bombs."

The mission began the following day. First, to avoid being located, the Hells Angels and their hired killers changed hotels. When planning a strike, the bikers left nothing to chance.

"Our team was in a red pickup, watching Gilles Lambert's house. I was with Frenchy, and two full-fledged Angels, J.C. and Paulo. We had revolvers and submachine guns. Day after day, we tried without success to spot Lambert. This was when Frenchy told me that several members of affiliated clubs were jealous because I had a choice position compared to them. I answered that the others only had to work as hard as I had. I had no hangups with respect to anybody. One night, when I was fed up with waiting for Lambert, I got out of the vehicle and walked towards our future victim's yard. I intended to shoot through the window if I spotted him. As I approached the fence, I changed my mind. Two huge dogs had started barking. I went back into the truck.

"After a few days of trying to corner Lambert, someone rang the alarm. The police were watching us. We discreetly returned to the hotel, and I informed the other teams. Rick was angry. The entire plan had just failed, and Frenchy got the whole blame since he'd moved a vehicle without asking Rick. That's when, according to Rick, the cops had spotted our group. Investigators were already watching the vehicle, which belonged to Fat Eddy, a member of the Jokers. After being bawled out by Rick, Frenchy had to go back to Trois-Rivières. Rick convened a meeting with the rest of us, and told us he'd decided to put a stop to everything. Fat Eddy was ordered to gather all the weapons and leave the premises without being seen. The Hells Angels didn't want all the guys to risk being arrested. I was disappointed at the turn of events, since I really had wanted to prove myself. And, besides, I also wanted the money. Better luck next time, I told myself."

(Later, QPF investigators went to the hotel and confirmed that the meeting took place by examining the footage recorded with surveillance cameras. On the videotape were all the men named by Quesnel.)

Meanwhile, another incident had taken place in Quebec City. Pit Caron had been arrested by QPF officers and charged with running a drug network for the Quebec City Hells Angels. Quesnel was surprised to hear that Caron had called on the services of a different lawyer this time. What Quesnel didn't know was that his good friend had just made a deal with the police. He had agreed to cooperate with them. Caron had even been released on bail, which many in the underworld found fishy, but not Quesnel. As far as he was concerned, he and Caron still had the job of killing Gino Hallé to carry out.

"Pit's girlfriend called, telling me to forget the job we were supposed to do. At first, I didn't understand what she meant. When Caron got out, he told me that the cops had bugged his vehicle and heard some of our conversations about Gino Hallé. I reassured him, saying that we'd wait a while, that he shouldn't worry. 'Anyhow,' I added, 'Hallé has so many enemies that if we don't kill him, someone else will.'"

The two friends parted, and Quesnel went back to tend to his business with Melou. The leader of the Trois-Rivières club seemed to like the killer's company more and more, even if Quesnel still had yet to carry out a single contract for the organization. He seemed to think that Quesnel was loyal and ready to do anything.

"I spent the better part of my time in Montreal's grand hotels. The Sheraton, the Meridien, and the Marriott. Rick Vallée was often with me. And since he enjoyed female company, we called on the services of escort agencies almost every night, always getting the most beautiful girls. We also met other people in those hotels, to negotiate drug deals for example. Melou did a lot of business there. And, we met with our spies, guys from the underworld who'd tell us about our enemies' activities.

"One morning, Mario came to see us. Melou had to go to the municipal court and we were to go along to protect him. When we got there, Damy and Frenchy were waiting for us as well. So Melou had good protection; only his lawyer was unarmed. Even Melou, who was sitting in the dock, had a pistol under his sweater. The war with the Rock Machine was starting at the time, and we were being very cautious since everyone had access to the record of appearances. The enemy could have set a trap for us. The proceedings were finally postponed, and we all ended up at a fancy Italian restaurant."

Quesnel enjoyed his early weeks with the Angels. Despite all these complications, the bikers took time to party. For the Hells Angels, the basics boil down to money, booze, sex, and drugs.

"The Angels drive around in luxury cars and like to show off. It was really impressive when we went out as a group. Imagine forty guys walking into a bar wearing their colours. The place would slowly empty. Once in a while a braggart would try to get near us. So we'd give him a warning, which was usually enough to convince him he should beat it. Naturally, those who insisted got a good hiding. And victims rarely lodged complaints. I saw some people get badly beaten up, with several bikers punching one guy. Members of puppet clubs, like the Blatnois, took care of security, both inside and outside. We were lords and masters in the bars we went to. If we weren't treated this way, the place would be torched."

During the winter of 1995, Le Gosier, a Trois-Rivières bar, was completely destroyed by fire. The public was dismayed. The establishment had been the meeting place for generations of students and had the reputation of being well administered. The violence of the blaze left no doubt that it was arson. Police never managed to solve the crime. However, they did know that the Hells Angels were mixed up in it. And Quesnel knew it as well.

"A few days before the fire, two Trois-Rivières prospects were furious at the bar owner for not allowing them to enter the premises wearing their colours. Shortly thereafter, while I was working inside the club's garage – sawing the bullets for my .44 magnum so they'd explode on impact – I saw one of the bikers take a cable. That cable was later found at the site of the blaze. They probably used it to climb onto the bar roof. In the hours that followed the fire, one of the two guys arrived at the clubhouse rather flustered and had an urgent private meeting with Melou. That night, during the TV newscast mentioning the fire, Melou was cracking jokes. In my mind, it's clear that the business over the colours was directly responsible for the fire."

And, of course, there were girls.

"Waitresses in the bars we frequented were generally very happy to see us, since they made a lot of money from us. Often, some waitress would leave the bar with one of us. Women like bikers. In fact, money is what they like. I've seen guys who were ugly as toads on the arms of beautiful women. Since they were Hells Angels, they were rich. We often brought girls back to the clubhouse. It wasn't unusual to see a procession of some fifteen cars, sometimes limousines, head toward the clubhouse. Once there, we transformed the place into a discotheque or strip club and the fun would begin. The women often ended up naked. I remember an evening in Grand-Mère, at the Blatnois clubhouse, when we drank plenty of booze. Girls took turns dancing on the bar, and many ended up in a clubhouse room with a biker."

Following those nights of debauchery, where massive quantities of alcohol and drugs were consumed, the bikers would get back to serious business. To maintain their lifestyle, they needed to make more and more money. At the time, Melou Roy was active in the drug business and Quesnel tagged along with him everywhere to provide protection. He was always armed. Roy met dealers from the Rock Machine in Montreal and managed to get a few of them to join his group by selling them drugs at a lower price. For these dealers, the added advantage of changing suppliers was an increased life expectancy.

"Melou would cut each kilogram of cocaine he got with two hundred grams of a neutral filler, whose only purpose was to increase the quantity of the drug. He earned about $7,000 for each kilogram he sold, and he'd easily sell several in a week. The profit was very good."

The Trois-Rivières chapter was in full expansion at the time, which provided the bikers with a great deal of confidence. Business was good, but they wanted more of it. And now war was raging; a war between the two groups over control of drug sales in certain territories, mostly in Quebec City and Montreal. In the Montreal area, hostilities barely allowed the belligerents any respite. At the beginning of 1995, the Hells Angels surprised many people when they decided to create an elite cell: the Nomads. This chapter had no home base, and its mandate was to conquer new territories, especially Ontario, where the Hells Angels did not control drug sales.

According to police lists at the beginning, the Nomads consisted of nine "soldiers." Among them were Louis "Melou" Roy and Rick Vallée from Trois-Rivières, and Maurice "Mom" Boucher, Denis "Pas Fiable" Houle, Normand "Biff" Hamel, Donald "Pup" Stockford, David "Nold" Carroll, Gilles "Trooper"

Mathieu, and Wolodumir "Nugget" Stadnick, all from the Montreal chapter.

"Melou and Rick were rather proud that the official address of the Nomads was that of the Trois-Rivières clubhouse. When the Nomads met, I was often chosen to provide security. It was during this time that Maurice 'Mom' Boucher, the leader of the Nomads, got six months in jail for possessing a firearm. As a result, the most important decisions were made by Melou. Members would meet pretty often, especially at the beginning."

Serge Quesnel watched, listened, and learned. He noticed that the bikers thought through everything before acting. If a decision was made to kill someone, the bikers always tried to ensure the operation was profitable. Victims often paid for their own murder.

"The Hells Angels aren't suckers. I noticed that before executing a criminal, the guys would often 'borrow' large quantities of drugs from him. As a result, they pocketed hundreds of thousands of dollars."

He also noticed that Melou often acted as though money didn't matter.

"One day, Rick told Melou that the police had found one of his cocaine stashes, the largest one, in fact. Melou started to laugh. I asked him if the hiding place contained a lot of drugs and he answered, 'Fifty or so kilos.' He'd often laugh to create the impression he was on top of things. When a lawyer asked him how much he'd lost,

Melou answered, 'About $1,300,000.' I was really sur-
prised. I thought that losing so much money was
serious. But all he was worried about was whether his
dealer had talked to the police. He asked the lawyer to
find out. Melou then set up a meeting with the guy who
had sold him the coke, wanting to find out whether he
was behind the police operation. The guy, who also
owned a Mercedes, was sufficiently reassuring, and
Melou agreed to absorb the loss."

The Angels' henchman didn't see his girlfriend often
any more. He called her once or twice a week, but he was
kept too busy to see her much. He observed how quickly
the Angels became serious when the situation demanded
it. He was given a good example of this during a meeting
set up by Melou, one that Frenchy and Nachos attended
as well. Quesnel was there with his friend Pit Caron. The
topic suddenly turned to the mission they were given:
killing Gino Hallé.

"Nachos still wanted us to honour the contract on
Hallé, and for the same money. He then asked Frenchy
and Pit to go to the ground floor of the clubhouse to
discuss the job further. I thought Nachos and Melou
had something to tell me about Pit, and I was right.
Melou told me that I was responsible for Pit's actions. I
quickly understood what he meant. If a guy ended up
in jail, especially a full-patch member like Nachos,
because of Pit, I'd be held accountable. The Angels

suspected Pit, and made it rather clear. In the days that followed, Nachos became very paranoid about Pit and wanted me to kill him. He was so paranoid that I was afraid for my own life. Nachos was without a doubt the most suspicious biker in the group. After a lengthy conversation, I finally convinced him that my buddy wasn't an informant. But I was wrong."

One night at the clubhouse, Roy walked over to Quesnel. The two men were alone. Roy wrote the name of Marcel Demers on a blackboard, asking Quesnel whether he knew him. His answer was no. Roy wrote, "Rock Machine, Quebec City, $15,000 to his killer." Just weeks earlier Melou had laughed when asked whether his clubhouse was bugged. But now the war was underway, he took no chances.

"Melou signalled me to follow him into the observation room to show me a photograph of Demers. He was older than we were and had a round face. I learned that he worked out at Gold's Gym on First Avenue in Quebec City. Melou mentioned that Demers did a lot of training on a stationary bike. This detail was important because the bikes were located behind the gym's windows. Melou added that it wasn't urgent because the Quebec City Hells Angels were also supposed to take care of him. Nonetheless, every time I went to Quebec City, I made a detour to First Avenue. I'd have killed Demers if I had ever seen him at Gold's Gym."

In May 2001, Marcel Demers was sentenced to nine years in jail. A founding member of the Rock Machine, who've since become the Bandidos, he pleaded guilty to seventeen charges related to a large cocaine and PCP network. Earlier, Demers survived several attempts on his life. The last one occurred in June 1999. While driving his car, he was hit by three bullets, from more than twenty fired by two men linked to the Quebec City Angels. The shooting took place through the streets of Beauport and Charlesbourg as the killers chased their prey. Despite his wounds, Demers managed to get to the l'Enfant-Jésus Hospital, where he was treated.

Quesnel, for his part, cheerfully travelled through this world of threats and strong-arm tactics. He liked the lifestyle the Angels imposed on him and although he knew he was walking the fine line between life and death every day, he didn't care. When the bikers have a good soldier, they do everything they can to keep him. And Quesnel was a good soldier, totally dedicated to the organization. So the bikers took care of him and made sure he didn't get bored. Outings, girls, money, nothing was spared to ensure the killer's interest remained on alert. He was hired to kill, and he soon had the opportunity to prove himself when Roy told him that Sudiste would give him a contract.

"Sudiste came to see me at the clubhouse in mid-December, two weeks before the guys were to leave for

holidays in Acapulco. We went into the ⟨
room and he asked me, in writing, whether I k⟨
Ferland. Since we didn't want to take the slightest risk,
in case the room was bugged, we often communicated
by writing rather than speaking. We used the blackboard
to write the key words. I signalled that I did. Then he
asked me to go with him to Grondines, where Ferland
lived, to do some reconnaissance work. The guy was a
major PCP manufacturer and sold his drugs to the Rock
Machine, the enemy. I knew Ferland, as I had been in
prison with him. The Angels wanted to kill him because
he was helping their enemy earn huge profits. Sudiste
offered me $10,000 to kill him on the understanding
that I would contribute $1,000 of that amount to the
Trois-Rivières chapter fund. I agreed.

"So we went to Grondines, and Sudiste showed me
Ferland's house, a white heritage building. After examining the place, I returned to Trois-Rivières. Sudiste
told me that my target probably drove around in a
truck. I had only seen a small car parked near the barn,
so after leaving Sudiste at the clubhouse, I went back to
Grondines to examine the site again, since I was determined to do a good job. This would be my first hit for
the Angels and I didn't want to fail. I wanted to take the
time needed to set up the murder properly. And I also
felt that the guys were testing me. At first, I studied the
different options for an escape route. I knew I'd kill

Ferland in his home, it was the best place. But doing surveillance day after day in such a small village wasn't easy. I didn't go unnoticed. A member of the Blatnois puppet club rented a Chrysler Intrepid for me. Not wanting to leave my name all over the place, I never rented cars myself."

For a few days, the killer tracked his prey. But Ferland was careful. Quesnel changed cars several times to make sure he wasn't spotted. He worried that he never saw Ferland's truck, and surmised that it didn't exist. To get to the bottom of things, he even went up to the house and knocked on the door, but no one answered. He also called on the services of an accomplice, Gaston, a former Donnacona inmate. Meeting him by accident in Quebec City, Quesnel offered him work as a driver.

"Gaston told me he needed money and was ready to do anything. He didn't seem to be bothered when I told him I needed his help to commit a murder. I offered him $1,500 for the job, and he was very happy. We worked a few days to set up the hit. Then, one night, we stole a car and headed for Grondines. Everything was ready. We had gloves and wigs and I had a 9 mm pistol. But Gaston was so nervous that he was shaking, and I could see he didn't feel too well. He was tense and not talking. We drove by Ferland's house a first time, and I saw him through the window. Ferland was a fat man, and the profile I'd just seen in the window left no doubt that it was him. But Gaston was shaking so badly, I thought he might stall the engine with the clutch. I tried to encourage him, telling him he was only the driver, but nothing worked. Gaston finally broke down, telling me he didn't want to go through with it. He wanted to return to Quebec City. I had no option but to let him back out. I was furious, but tried not to show it."

Gaston today must consider himself lucky not to have taken part in the murder. However, that day, on the return trip, he was terribly ill at ease. He hadn't fulfilled his contract and knew that Quesnel was seething. Gaston was aware that he knew too much, and that where the Hells Angels were involved, there was little hope for mercy.

"On the way back, Gaston was worried. And with reason. I asked him if he was afraid of going to hell. After I made serious threats, he assured me he'd keep his mouth shut. I was stuck with an embarrassing witness, and told him we knew his brother and father, that he'd better lie low if he didn't want them to have an accident. But deep down, I knew I'd probably have to get rid of him sooner or later."

So the plan failed. A few days before Christmas, several Trois-Rivières bikers, including Roy, left for Acapulco. Quesnel was told he would be able to join them once he had killed Ferland. Louis Roy had rented a villa for the sum of $40,000 a month. Other bikers would be staying at the prestigious Princess Hotel. All they wanted was to have fun. Twenty-two bikers flew to Mexico on family vacation with their wives and children. Besides Roy, the travellers included Dan, Nachos, Sudiste, and Paulo. Quesnel had to act quickly if he wanted to go there as well. He contacted Pit Caron.

"Since I wanted the job done, and since I trusted Pit, I offered him $5,000. He asked about a few details, and we went over to Grondines to check out the place. Pit accepted the contract and seemed satisfied. While we were chatting, he even had a good idea, suggesting we steal a car to commit the crime and make our escape. Farther on we would dump the car, pick up a snowmobile, and continue along the trails. The cops would never find us. We could make our way to Val-Bélair, north of Quebec City. But the plan required a little patience: we had to wait for the rivers to freeze since there would be many of them along our route."

In the following days, however, Jack Ferland dropped out of sight. Quesnel and Caron concluded that he had also gone south for a holiday. To avoid wasting too much time while waiting for him to return, Quesnel told his friend they should find Gino Hallé instead, and kill him.

"Pit agreed. I knew he knew Hallé, but what I didn't know was that he was really good friends with him. I found out later that he warned Hallé that we were after him. So Hallé asked for police protection, and the QPF found him a hiding place in Montreal for a while. In the meantime, Caron spent his days with me looking for Hallé. He was a very good actor, and I didn't suspect a thing. We went around in circles, but Hallé couldn't be found. We continued looking for a few days, then gave up. At the time, Pit had lost control of his cocaine habit. He was using a lot and no longer took good care of his business. I should have talked to him about the problem, but I didn't want to face facts either. He was quickly degenerating. His wife tried to reason with him. I think he knew that his criminal life was coming to an end. When I'd see him completely stoned, Nachos's suspicion that he was an informant would come back to me. The thought of killing him crossed my mind a few times, but I always dismissed the idea.

"Much later on, when I was in a Quebec City strip bar, Hallé came in with another guy. The advantage I had was that he didn't know me. I was armed and, for a moment, thought of killing him in the bar. But I held back because I was with a friend who wasn't really a criminal. We left the bar and, to my surprise, Hallé and his friend walked into the elevator with us. I had a huge adrenalin rush. Touching the butt of my revolver, I was just itching to knock him off. But I had to keep telling myself not to, since I didn't want to involve my friend. Now Gino Hallé will know he came really close to dying that day."

The year 1995 began badly for Quesnel, when Chantal put an end to their relationship. She hated his frequent absence and could no longer tolerate his aggressiveness.

"I was pretty intense at the time. Besides all the rest, I was taking steroids without training, which really affected my mood. A few days before we broke up, I'd pointed my revolver at Chantal for no reason. Though I spoke to her loudly, I never hit her. I was a real pain when I lost my cool, and had once even thrown my dog off the third storey of a building in Limoilou. Nose had told his sister, 'You're lucky it wasn't you.' After learning over the phone that she was leaving me, I went to a bar to talk to her about her decision, but she'd already left. It was over."

During his time with the bikers, Serge Quesnel stayed in touch with his mother. He tried to reassure her, as she was very worried about him. She knew he was now working for the Hells Angels, but not in what capacity. He understood her anxiety but, for him, there was no turning back. One day, his mother showed up at the Trois-Rivières clubhouse, but refused to walk in. She was scared. Quesnel gave her a used car. But she was powerless to prevent his descent into hell.

The rest of Quesnel's family didn't hear much from him. It had already been a few years since he last saw his father.

"He'd call me three times a year," says Quesnel senior. "I knew he was with the bikers, although I didn't know where. He'd call me on New Year's Day, on my birthday, and on his birthday. The calls were always from a phone booth. I'd try to find out how he was and he'd always say he was doing well. I'd urge him to leave the bikers, telling him he'd get into trouble, but he wouldn't hear of it. His brother had also tried to reason with him, to no avail. He was really committed."

The Hells Angels vacationing in Mexico suddenly returned to Canada. Normand Baker, an important member of the Rock Machine, had been shot at point-blank range in an Acapulco café on January 4, 1995. The thirty-four-year-old Baker was murdered in a packed restaurant, where he was dining with his wife and another couple. François Hinse, who was linked to the Trois-Rivières Hells Angels, was apparently the one who pumped several bullets into Baker. Hinse tried to escape by jumping through a window, but the waiters reacted quickly, running outside and overpowering him with some difficulty. Mexican police from a station across the street intervened and arrested Hinse.

"Melou immediately took everyone back to Quebec, not wanting the police to start questioning their wives and children. He didn't want the Mexican police to pay too much attention to the Hells Angels. When the guys came back, they told me not to be too worried about François. Contacts were already being approached to get him out. They were saying he'd be acquitted, but that it would take a few weeks. With François Hinse behind bars, I was the group's number-one henchman."

On January 17, 1995, as though by magic, the Mexican court hearing the Hinse case dropped the proceedings. Judge Edmundo Roman Pinzon disregarded the testimonies of several witnesses to the murder, among them waiters and customers of the restaurant, as well as Baker's wife, Linda Perron, and her friend Valérie Lussier. According to a Mexican journalist, a $700,000 bribe was given to get Hinse acquitted. José Antonio Sanchez, from the *Diario* newspaper, asked why the judge hadn't considered testimony about Hinse following Baker on a motorcycle the morning of the day preceding the murder. The affair created such a scandal in Mexico that the country's legal officials decided to investigate the judge's actions. New charges were immediately brought against the Trois-Rivières biker. Hinse faced a jail term of up to thirty years. However, at the end of proceedings that lasted a little more than a year, Roger Bellemare, a lawyer from Trois-Rivières, managed to get François Hinse released while denouncing the RCMP for having pressured the Mexican government to convict his client.

In the meantime, Quesnel continued to plot the murder of Jacques Ferland. Some Angels were beginning to feel that things were dragging on. Paulo questioned Quesnel, showing his impatience. But Quesnel reassured him: the temperature had to drop before he could carry out his plan. But, by then, it was already very cold.

"I'll probably never forget Sunday, January 29, 1995. Everything was ready, the waterways were frozen, and I went to pick up the stolen vehicle. We'd left it in the parking lot of the Laval University Hospital in Quebec City, so it wouldn't be noticed and could easily be retrieved. Pit, meanwhile, went to pick up the snowmobile. We'd agreed to meet near Ferland's house in a spot where wood was being cut. The area could be reached by a concession road that led to a clearing where heavy machinery was located. I arrived before Pit and waited for him behind a log pile that was higher than the car. I was thinking about our plan and wasn't too nervous. Pit arrived about five minutes later, having stopped in Saint-Marc-des-Carrières to fill the snowmobile's gas tank.

"We'd slipped large jogging pants over our ski suits to conceal our identities. Any witnesses spotting us would likely describe us as being larger than we were. Besides, they wouldn't see our ski outfits. I wore gloves and a toque. Pit was ready. He had a nickel-plated

.357 magnum, with four bullets in the cylinder. He took the wheel. Meanwhile, seated on the passenger side, I pulled out my weapon for a final check, carefully wiping off all fingerprints. Pit started the car and we left the clearing. As we reached Ferland's house, we spotted a small car that was about to pull out of the entrance. 'Block his way,' I told Pit. The adrenalin, of course, was starting to rush. All my senses were heightened. In Ferland's yard, adding to the suspense, a tethered dog was barking continuously."

"The man who came out of the vehicle wasn't Ferland. Thinking quickly, I asked, 'Is Jack there? Yoland, from Quebec City, has sent me to see him.' I knew that Ferland had a contact with that name. It came to me in a flash. The man answered, 'Wait a minute. I'll get him.' As he was heading toward the house, I told Pit, 'If the guy returns, hold him back.' I got out of the car, heading the same way as Ferland's friend. At the door of the house, the dog was so close that he nearly bit me. Once inside, I walked down a dark hallway leading to a well-lit dining room. I heard the man [André Bédard, twenty-nine years old, one of Ferland's accomplices in the drug business] say to Ferland, 'There are two guys downstairs who want to see you.'

" 'Did you let them in?'

" 'No, they're in a car.'

"'Go and tell them to wait. I'll come down.'

"I was hiding near the dining room, holding my revolver, ready to shoot. Standing in a dark corner, leaning against a wall, I heard Bédard's footsteps approaching. Had he seen me, I'd have pressed the weapon against his head and signalled him to keep quiet. But he didn't; he walked right beside me as he headed back outside. I went through the dining room and hid in the adjoining kitchenette, from where I had a good view of the stairs. Ferland was on the second floor. I could hear him. Then I saw legs walking down the stairs, and pointed my gun in that direction. Jacques Ferland was in front, and I could see, behind him, the legs of a woman also coming down the stairs. I fired. Two bullets hit Ferland, who collapsed against the wall before tumbling down the stairs. There was a lot of blood. I was hoping the woman would run up the stairs to get away; otherwise I'd have to shoot her. Luckily, she did run back up, screaming. As I was about to escape, Bédard came back into the house and grabbed my right arm. But I'm left-handed and so I didn't have any difficulty shooting him in the chest. He collapsed at my feet. I then walked up to Ferland, who was stretched out, his head near the bottom of the stairs. He was moaning. I fired a bullet into his head. He was dead, I was sure of it. The woman's screams were heart-rending, and I was in a hurry to get out of there. Since I was sure that Ferland was dead, I went over to Bédard, leaned over, and fired my last bullet into his head.

"At that moment, Pit came storming into the house, holding his .357 magnum. He'd heard the shots and was wondering if I'd been hit. He stumbled onto a very sorry sight. Two corpses lay in the hall, and a horrible smell of blood and gunpowder filled the air. There was a lot of blood. It was awful. We left the house and got into the car. The road was slippery, and Pit, likely a little nervous, was driving too quickly. I asked him to slow down, since this really wasn't the time to drive into the ditch. I then tossed my 9 mm pistol and the spare magazine out the window. The adrenalin was still rushing through me, but a feeling of pride was gradually coming over me. I'd been plotting this hit for such a long time. Now I could finally tell my bosses that the job was done, and was really anxious to give them the news. As we were driving, I took off my camouflage clothes and put them in a backpack. We reached the clearing where the snowmobile was. I wasn't too worried about ditching the car there as it couldn't be seen from the road. We hid it behind a pile of logs, where the police weren't soon likely to find it. I was sure they wouldn't think we'd escaped on a snowmobile.

"Fortunately, the snowmobile started without a glitch, but the ride was awful. Besides being long, it was murder on my back. On reaching Val-Bélair, we went over to the home of one of Pit's friends, where we left the snow-mobile. Another man picked us up and drove us to Pit's place, where we put our clothes in a bag. I took a quick shower to remove any powder I might have on my skin. I was sure I could smell it. Our driver then took us to the Laval University Hospital, where I picked up my car. I thanked him and drove off. Shortly afterwards, I ditched the clothes in a large container located in a restaurant parking lot on Laurier Boulevard in Quebec City."

But instead of driving far away, Serge Quesnel returned to the scene of the crime. Caron had lost a roll of tape along the way that certainly had his fingerprints on it, and Quesnel didn't want the cops to find it.

"I was heading back to Trois-Rivières, but decided to look for the tape. I took the Grondines exit off Highway 40, and drove by Ferland's house. Contrary to what I expected, there were no cops. Just yellow police tape around the perimeter of the crime scene. Pit was sure he'd left the tape in the stolen car, so I went back to it. Since everything in the area seemed calm, I pulled up to the car and searched it thoroughly. I couldn't find the tape. I was getting desperate, looking all around the car. Nothing. So I left."

What Quesnel didn't know at the time he was planning the murder was that his victim, the forty-two-year-old Ferland, was about to be arrested. Police from the Montreal Urban Community wanted to put him out of commission. They'd found a lot of evidence that he was making and distributing PCP. Ferland's wife was sentenced for this shortly after his murder, as was André Bédard, the man whom Quesnel shot twice, including once in the head. Despite these wounds, staff at Quebec City's Saint-François-d'Assise Hospital managed to save his life. After Ferland's murder, the QPF's personal crimes division discovered chemicals inside his house that could be used to make up to seventy kilos of PCP. Chemists who they called to the site concluded that another seventy kilos had already been made by the traffickers. Nine people were arrested.

"I drove back to Trois-Rivières and headed directly to the Hells Angels' clubhouse. I was tired, and the tension I felt was slowly easing. That night, I had no trouble falling asleep. I had no remorse. I felt like a soldier at war. When I woke up, I saw the newspaper headline: "SHOOTING IN GRONDINES," and quickly read the article. I was shocked to read that Bédard had survived. He was now in a position to identify me, and I couldn't try anything as he was under tight security. Then Melou arrived. He was in a good mood and reassured me, saying that if anything happened, the Angels would take care of it, adding that Bédard's recollection probably had a few good holes in it. We laughed. Melou told me to relax and not worry. He asked Sudiste to pay me the $10,000, saying Ferland's death was well worth it. Sudiste gave me the amount in twenty-dollar bills. Melou even exempted me from paying the $1,000 earmarked for the clubhouse's operating fund. He was very pleased with the job. I gave Pit his share."

Quesnel was proud of himself. After all, his mission had succeeded; he had killed Ferland. But he didn't know whether he was being blamed for leaving a survivor behind. So he watched everything the bikers did, not wanting to be the next target. The fear soon passed. Quesnel played his role well. Now he was *the* killer for the organization, the man ready to take all risks for the Hells Angels. He was pumped. War was raging and the Rock Machine had to be shaken up. Quesnel had just proved beyond any doubt that he was totally dedicated to the Hells Angels. They weren't about to let him cool down.

"We began watching Serge Quesnel in January 1995, following Jacques Ferland's murder," says Insp. Pierre Frenette. "We knew he was working for the Trois-Rivières Hells Angels and that he wasn't one of them. I spent a great deal of time following him myself. We were starting to refine the plan of attack we'd devised within the framework of Project Nordic."

The goal of the QPF's Project Nordic was to arrest and charge leaders of the Trois-Rivières Hells Angels. At

that time, Quesnel didn't suspect that the police were
following him.

"One morning, shortly after Ferland's murder, Rick
Vallée and a few other bikers arrived at the Trois-
Rivières clubhouse. They wanted me to go along with
them to find out about my next mission. So we drove
to Le Gardeur, on the outskirts of Montreal. Rick
wanted to show me the house of Luc Deschênes, nicknamed BF, for *beau-frère* [brother-in-law]. He was a
former contract killer himself, but I didn't know him.
He was a member of the Dark Circle, an organization
opposed to the Hells Angels, and I was being offered
$25,000 to kill him. The l'Assomption River flowed
right behind Deschênes's house, which gave us the idea
of using boats to attack him. We were joking around,
but I still observed the site carefully and told them to
let me know when they were ready.

"We then headed to Montreal, where Melou was
waiting for us at the Mikado restaurant. When I arrived,
my boss gave me a wad of twenty-dollar bills, which
amounted to some $2,000. He was acting as though
the money were burning a hole in his pockets. This
suited me fine. Melou often behaved that way. He didn't
want me to run out of money. A happy killer is a pro-
ductive killer. At times, I'd have $6,000 in pocket money.
I felt rich and powerful. The Hells Angels value murders
and other crimes. Full-patch members kept encouraging

me, saying I'd be one of them some day. Colours are very important to them. I knew that even if I became their best killer, I'd only be their equal the day I got my colours. And I wanted them."

At the beginning of February, Melou Roy called Quesnel, saying he wanted to meet him at the Rowdy Crew clubhouse in Lavaltrie as soon as possible. Rick Vallée drove him there.

"When we arrived, only le Flo Lussier was there. We were somewhat acquainted, and talked about this and that. Le Flo had also gone to the Rowdy Crew clubhouse on Melou's orders. He told me he knew a girl in Quebec City who hung out with members of the Rock Machine, and that he was planning to grill her just to see if he could get information. He wanted the addresses of a few guys, and told me we were to carry out a contract together. It looked as though Melou had found me a partner. All the members of the affiliated groups knew I was a killer for Melou, which is to say, for the Nomads. I was aware that le Flo was also a killer for the organization. He'd been acquitted of a murder a few years earlier.

"Melou arrived about an hour late, accompanied by a prospect called Mario. He immediately told us he needed a job done. 'You'll be working together. Mario will tell you all about it tomorrow. The job will earn you $15,000, which you'll have to share.' Mario and he then quickly left the clubhouse, looking a little stressed.

"Le Flo suggested I sleep at his place, and I was glad. I didn't really like the Rowdy Crew clubhouse. I thought it was in poor taste. Located beside Highway 40, it resembled a low-end medieval castle. It had four turrets, inside which were the bedrooms; tiny rooms with a bed, a desk, and a mirror. I much preferred to stay at Lussier's.

"The next day, Mario came to get us. He wanted to show us where our target lived. So he took us to the home of Claude 'le Pic' Rivard. It was a nice, Canadian-style house, with a TEMPO shelter going all the way to the street. Mario described le Pic to us, saying he was a rather small man with long brown hair. He drove around in a convertible Pontiac Bonneville, while his wife had a small white Suzuki. He also told us that le Pic could be found at Bar 45, on Broadway Street.

"Since I didn't know Montreal very well, it was Lussier's job to plan our escape. We had problems with the cars we stole to do the hit, twice having to find new vehicles. Then we began our surveillance. After a few hours, I spotted a suspicious-looking truck that had just been parked a short distance up the same street. I mentioned it to Lussier, so we decided to check it out. You can imagine how surprised I was to see Flat, a Trois-Rivières biker covered with tattoos, inside the truck. Then, as we drove around the street corner, we came face to face with Dan and Serge, two other Angels. They looked pretty surprised as well. We agreed to head to a bowling alley parking lot to talk things over. The guys told us that they were tracking another target, and agreed to let us carry on with our job. But things weren't working out. We were there for a few days and never saw le Pic. As had happened many times since the beginning of this mission, Lussier contacted Mario, who was Melou's right-hand man for this business. Mario suggested we get le Pic at his hangout, Bar 45, instead. He even drew a map to show us where the bar was located. So off we went.

"Lussier walked into the bar to see if le Pic was there. He was. Lussier came back to our truck and we waited. We had hoods to conceal our faces. We saw him leave the bar and then return, and leave again in the middle of the afternoon. This time we followed him. My feeling is that Claude Rivard knew he was being followed. He made several detours to try to shake us. On reaching Notre-Dame Street, I asked Lussier if this was a good place to shoot him, and he said yes. We caught up to Rivard's car when it stopped at a red light. I got out of the truck, waving my magnum. I shot the first bullet into his eye. He was wearing a seat belt, so his body fell to the side, but then moved back to an upright position. I fired again before climbing back into the truck. Lussier pressed the accelerator, but then we were stopped by a police cruiser a few metres away.

"'What do we do?' Lussier asked.

" 'Run for it!'

"A chase worthy of the best police films then began. I tossed my weapon out the window, then heard a loud noise. The glass of a bus shelter had just shattered. No doubt thinking that I was shooting at people, the cops chasing us slowed down a little. Lussier gave me his weapon, telling me to get rid of it, which I did after quickly wiping the fingerprints off. More and more cops were on our tail and I was nervous. A police car crashed behind us, and we drove on, soon reaching a residential neighbourhood. At one point, things were almost comical. We drove down a dead end, and came across several police cars after we backtracked. A little farther on, we managed to get a small lead, and decided to ditch the car and escape on foot. I told Lussier, 'You go your way, I'll go mine, and good luck!' I didn't go very far. A few metres from where we'd left the truck, I spotted a house with a raised balcony, and decided to dive underneath it. Since there was a little snow on the ground, I didn't want the cops to find me by following my tracks. I'd found a good hiding spot, and in the following seconds I heard a cop ask a child if he'd seen two men running. The child's answer seemed to indicate a direction, which reassured me somewhat. But the game wasn't over.

"I was under the balcony, literally freezing. But there was still a lot of action in the area, and there was no way

I was going to leave my hideout. After an hour, I was so cold that I had to climb out, otherwise, I'd have frozen to death. I was only wearing a sweatshirt and a black jean jacket. I was completely lost, as I didn't know Montreal at all. Still, I had to do something. While under the balcony, I'd heard the sound of a bus come by every fifteen minutes or so. As it happened, the bus arrived just as I came out of my lair. I took the precaution of pretending to wave farewell to the people in the house, in case police were watching, and got on the bus. I warmed up gradually, and noticed that my clothes were covered in dirt and dead leaves. I carefully brushed off as much as I could, then got off the bus after a few minutes. Bingo! I ended up right in the middle of the police roadblock. I kept my cool and vanished into the crowd. I hopped into the first cab I saw, asking the driver to take me to the Berri-UQAM subway station. I didn't really know what I was going to do. When I got there, I found a little motel and went to buy new clothes. Since I was pretty sure I'd managed to shake the cops, I wasn't really afraid. Back at the motel, I took a shower, put all the clothes I'd worn during the murder into a bag, and tossed it into a large container. Only five days after killing Ferland, I'd just killed le Pic Rivard. Things were decidedly moving quickly."

Serge Quesnel's accomplice, le Flo Lussier, however, was arrested. Police·nabbed him quickly after the two men split up. After contacting Melou Roy, Quesnel got a call from Mario, asking that he join him and Rick Vallée at a Chinese restaurant. They decided that Quesnel should hide in a hotel near the Olympic Stadium, the kind of place where it's easy to register under an assumed name. While going to pick up the few things Quesnel had left at le Flo's place, Mario was stopped for a routine check. The cops taunted him, saying they knew he was behind Rivard's murder. They took him to the station, but he was released twenty-four hours later. Quesnel eventually made his way to the Trois-Rivières clubhouse after hiding out for forty-eight hours. He was given a warm welcome.

"Melou was happy to see me. This whole business had stressed him. The other guys were there as well. They all laughed when I told them my story, especially at the part about catching a cold under the balcony. Melou paid up, handing me five bundles of $2,000 each, all of them tied together. I told Melou that he owed me $7,500, as agreed, not $10,000. He answered that my work was worth the money he was giving me. Melou was beside the pool table, which was covered with money. Rick was there as well, along with a guy named Denis. He's the one who showed up with the money, which was in a cardboard box. Denis had a territory in the Outaouais, where he sold drugs for the Trois-Rivières bikers. Melou and Rick were counting the money as Denis looked on. I was in the kitchen when Rick came to join me about a half-hour later. He told me that Denis had just tried to screw them out of $400,000. Going over to the blackboard, he wrote down that he was my next contract. I told him that I could kill him right away, but he refused, saying he wanted Denis to pay his debts before I murdered him. The guy had a very lucrative territory, and Rick led me to understand that I could inherit that 'business opportunity.'

"A few days later, I saw Denis and Rick again, at a Dunkin' Donuts in Montreal. He'd just paid a lot of money back to Rick. As he left the doughnut shop, Rick told me that Denis was in the process of paying for his funeral. I felt I was now part of the gang. The guys wanted to take me along more and more often. A few days later, Dan asked me to go with him.

"'Come on. We're going to buy a bike.'

'What?'

'You'll need one next summer.'

"I was surprised and pleased by Dan's way of doing things. At the dealer's, he asked me to choose the motorcycle I liked best. He suggested the Road King model, but I opted for the Wild Glide instead. I forked out $10,000 for the bike. Had Dan not helped, I'd have had to wait until I had enough money to buy the superb machine. I was already anxious to ride it."

In early February 1995, in order to have a little fun and get ready for the next motorbike season, several bikers headed for the Saguenay, where an exhibition of Harley bikes was taking place against a backdrop of rock music. It was also an excuse to party. Serge Quesnel was part of the crowd there, as were a majority of Hells Angels and dozens of members from affiliated groups.

"We'd rented the entire Roussillon hotel and were still short of rooms. Since I was Melou's killer, I stayed with him in his suite. And Melou always had the nicest room. There were so many of us that it was scary. Before heading over to the exhibition, we had a meeting at the clubhouse of the Satan's Guards, the Hells Angels' puppet club in the region. Following a brief meeting, we headed to the exhibition, which was taking place inside an arena. Event organizers gave us the best spots for the show. Bikers love to discover new Harley models – as well as the beautiful girls who parade around with them. Later that evening we ended up in a bar. At one point, Melou drew my attention to a man who was seated at the bar, saying, 'Look at him carefully, he's gonna get a damn good beating.' Seconds later, two large bikers from affiliated clubs walked up to him and severely beat him. He had the misfortune of being in the wrong place at the wrong time."

That night, Quesnel became better acquainted with the Quebec City Hells Angels. While everyone was partying, he was hailed by two full-patch members of the Quebec City chapter. One was named Sauvage. Quesnel had seen him speaking with Roy earlier in the evening. He had also noticed that the two men were continually looking at him, but hadn't been able to hear what they were saying. He would soon find out what was behind those funny looks.

"A waitress in a Limoilou bar says you work for the police," Sauvage told him.

"'What?'

Melou Roy had drawn near and was listening carefully. The accusation was serious. It could have cost Quesnel his life if he was found guilty. And in this kind of trial, conducted by the bikers, a doubt, even a reasonable one, isn't enough to spare the defendant's life.

"The waitress said you were in the bar thirty seconds before a police raid. That you threw down a cigarette pack with cocaine in it before leaving. And that you avoided the police raid as though by magic. It's fishy."

"I've never collaborated with the cops. That's not my style. I don't know what you're talking about."

At that point, Roy intervened: "I've known Sergio for a long time and he's not the type. Leave him alone. In a year, he'll have killed a dozen people for us. Do you guys in Quebec City have anyone like him?"

"That was the end of the matter," Quesnel says. "It even helped me get a little closer to the Quebec City guys. As for what they'd said I'd done, I remembered being in the bar they mentioned, and they were even right about the cigarette pack. I'd got drunk that night and had bought a few grams of cocaine in a spot controlled by the Rock Machine, where nobody knew me. I'd done this to make sure my bosses wouldn't criticize me, since they didn't like it when their men did coke. Toward the end of the evening, I was really smashed and threw the cigarette pack on the floor. I hadn't remembered that cocaine was in it. I hadn't seen it. But there was no way I was involved with the cops. It was only a coincidence.

"A little later in the evening, after my encounter with the Quebec City bikers, Melou came to see me and suggested that I get revenge.

"'You should kill that waitress,' he said.

"'Yeah,' I answered, thinking him a little harsh.

"In fact, he was right. By uttering such nonsense, the girl might have got me killed. The place was filled with bikers that night, and those guys don't kid around with informants. If Melou hadn't intervened, I don't know what would've happened. So I decided to give the waitress a really good scare. One afternoon, a few days later, I went to the Évasion bar, where she worked. She was alone, and as soon as I walked in I saw fear in her eyes. I purposely kept my gloves on to let her know I was armed.

"'So. I'm a cop, eh?' I asked.

"'No, no, that's not what I meant . . .'

"'Put your coat on, you're coming with me.'

"'No, don't hurt me.'

"'Put on your coat, we're going to the Angels' club-house in Quebec City. You're gonna tell them you made a mistake.'

"'Don't worry. Tonight, everyone will know the truth about you. I promise. Leave me here. I can't leave the bar. You'll see. Trust me.'

"I agreed. The girl couldn't stop thanking me. I don't know what she said to the Quebec City guys, but the message got all the way to Trois-Rivières. And my honour was saved. Melou never mentioned the issue again. He didn't care much for the Quebec City Hells Angels anyhow. A few weeks later, during a party, the president of the Quebec City chapter offered me the colours of his club. I declined, since I felt I was getting closer to the Nomads. I was aiming for the top. When Melou heard the news, he burst out laughing. He claimed that the Quebec City Hells Angels were country bumpkins and not very resourceful, adding, 'They don't even have enough money to support you.' The Quebec City guys never understood why I didn't want to work for them."

Quesnel's life of debauchery continued. One party followed the other, as did murderous plans.

"One afternoon, while we were at the clubhouse, Flat, one of the Nomads, mentioned Tit-Os Trudel to me. He wrote his name on the blackboard and gave me a sheet of paper with Trudel's photo on it that had been taken from a Laval police album. As a bonus, it also had all the necessary information about the man, courtesy of the cops. Flat told me the guy was a Rock Machine hit man, and that I'd earn $25,000 for killing him. But he was unable to tell me where Trudel lived. Apparently he moved around a lot. A few days later, while I was with Pit Caron at the Carol Club in Quebec City, I showed him the picture, saying that the contract on him would be very lucrative. Pit said he didn't know him, and he suggested I remove the Laval police logo from the sheet of paper, to avoid problems if I were ever caught with it."

Even though the Angels love to party, Quesnel knew that he must never forget why he was there: to kill. Between contracts, however, he still managed to take advantage of the bikers' wealth.

"One morning, while I was at the Trois-Rivières clubhouse, Melou called and told me to meet him in Montreal at a luxury-car dealership, located across from the hippodrome. In his view, it was time for us to treat ourselves and change cars. Rick Vallée came to join us. The lot contained the most expensive cars: Lamborghinis, Mercedes, Jaguars, Ferraris, and Bentleys. The salesman was in seventh heaven. Between the three of us, we spent $350,000. Melou bought a twelve-cylinder, black Mercedes 600 SL convertible for $170,000, while Rick and I each got an $86,000 Jaguar. There were only two Jaguars on the lot, one black, the other salmon coloured. Rick gave me the first pick and I jumped on the black one. Vallée had class. Mario then joined us. He decided to buy Melou's 'old' Mercedes 500 SL, for $80,000. I had to leave my new car on the lot as I didn't have a driver's licence. Melou absolutely wanted me to get one. That way, the insurance would pay for the car if I had an accident. A member of the Blatnois was to take care of getting me a licence. But time was against me."

A man doesn't get such a gift without having to do something in return. Serge Quesnel was in wide demand among the bikers. There were several men they wanted him to kill: Tit-Os Trudel; René Guillet, from La Tuque; Robert Dubuc, president of the Jokers, a club affiliated to the Hells Angels; Stéphane Paré, owner of a bar in the Upper Mauricie; and Denis Plante, a drug dealer in the Outaouais region.

"Sudiste asked me to kill René Guillet. The Hells Angels were upset with him for selling drugs for the Rock Machine. He was no longer taking warnings seriously and, moreover, Sudiste didn't like his face. It's hard to imagine being in a worse position. Sudiste contacted me at the clubhouse, asking that I go with him to Grand-Mère. As we were climbing into my car, he asked me for a piece of paper to write on. All I had on me was the photocopy of Trudel's picture. Sudiste took it and wrote René Guillet's name on the back. He was offering me $10,000 to kill Guillet.

"We drove for an hour and a half to La Tuque. Once we got there, Sudiste headed into a rock bar he knew. He came out with two guys who showed us the location of René Guillet's, his mother's, and his girlfriend's homes. They also showed us the gym where Guillet trained. Sudiste then asked one of the guys who owned a cottage to get it ready for me, along with clothing and food. As we were driving back to Trois-Rivières, I remembered a detail: a For Sale sign was planted in front of Guillet's house. I told Sudiste I'd have to return to La Tuque to take down the number on the sign. I already had a plan in mind: I'd call Guillet to visit his house, and once we were in the basement, I'd kill him. It was quick and easy, and Sudiste agreed. Next day, the two of us went to a garage to meet Stanley, a guy who worked for the Angels and hid weapons for the Trois-Rivières bikers. He handed me a gun, then walked away. Afterwards, I returned to La Tuque and jotted down the phone number."

Making an appointment with Guillet to see his house might have been a good idea, but it didn't work. Quesnel called several times, but no one ever answered.

In the meantime, Quesnel accompanied the Angels to a boxing match. Bikers like boxing, and the Hells

Angels always show up in large numbers at matches. They take advantage of these outings to show off their colours and brawn. These are also good opportunities to talk about business. Inside the Chicoutimi sports centre, during a boxing match between Alain Bonnamie and Stéphane Ouellet, Quesnel became reacquainted with members of other clubs. He also saw the lawyer who set him up with the Hells Angels.

"There were about a hundred and twenty of us guys there that time. The best places around the ring were reserved for the Hells Angels, while the guys from affiliated clubs were scattered throughout the crowd. This was the usual arrangement and it often led to fights with spectators who had the misfortune of getting mixed up with the bikers' games. All the guys wore their large rings, which not only glitter, but hurt as well. Bikers often use them as weapons. That night, in Chicoutimi, the guys were drinking heavily, and tempers flared pretty quickly. At one point, the lawyer asked me to 'take care' of Roger Aubin. I'd met Aubin at Donnacona, where he was still imprisoned. Thinking he'd been poorly defended, he wanted to get even with the lawyer because he'd been sentenced to twenty-five years. The lawyer was sitting in the first row with Dan, the vice-president of the Trois-Rivières Angels, while I was in the third row with Serge Tremblay and his girlfriend. I knew the lawyer was really worried about Aubin. He told me that, on a recent Florida vacation, he'd been unable to sleep because he was so concerned about this business. I could tell he was scared and I teased him.

"Following the boxing match, we went to a discotheque. I was quietly seated at the bar, looking at girls, when the lawyer came to join me. He ordered two B-52s, and after asking whether I'd enjoyed the match, he told me that Aubin would soon be appealing his sentence.

"'I'll have problems if he gets out, as you know. Can you knock him off?'

"'Are you serious?'

"'I don't care what it costs. Do it for me.'

"'Don't worry, I won't let you down. I'll take care of it and we can talk about the details later.'

"'I'll ask Melou for you to come and stay at my place if Aubin is released. I'm not like you guys. This really bothers me!'

"After that, he treated me to B-52s the whole evening, and I got really sick, throwing up everywhere. I slept at the Satan's Guards clubhouse, while the other guys from Trois-Rivières stayed in hotels. When I left the next morning for Trois-Rivières, I had a really bad hangover. I rather liked my lawyer. I'd known about him since 1991. A friend had recommended him after I was arrested for the holdup of a credit union in Saint-Émile. At the time, I'd decided not to use his services. Later on, while I was in jail, several guys told me he was a good lawyer, and I got to know him in 1993. I went over to his place to say hello a few days following the boxing match. He introduced me to his wife, saying, 'He's the guy I got smashed on B-52s with.' As I was about to leave his place, he slipped a word to me: 'Don't forget about Aubin.'"

The QPF is certain that Quesnel is telling the truth about this contract. They filed a case with the Crown Attorney's Office so that the lawyer would be charged with conspiracy. According to a police officer who followed the case closely, an influential member of the Department of Justice intervened to prevent the lawyer from being brought before the court.

Killing Aubin wasn't the only contract Quesnel was being offered. "The Hells Angels were targeting a man from the Upper Mauricie, Stéphane Paré, a hotel-keeper in the small town of Rivière-à-Pierre. Paré had to die because he'd once shot at some bikers. I have a good recollection of the conversation I had about Paré with my accomplice for this hit, a Blatnois biker. He and I had agreed to steal a car in Quebec City, then hide it somewhere before doing the hit. I didn't have a very good description of Paré, and my accomplice said we could get one at the clubhouse of the Quebec City Hells Angels, who kept all the back issues of *Allô Police*. He said he remembered seeing Paré's photo in the newspaper. And we did, in fact, find it. My accomplice had a good memory.

"During that visit to the Quebec City Angels 'library,' two full-patch members asked me to kill Michel 'Jim' Comeau and Éric Pelletier, two members of the Rock Machine. Melou had already asked me to kill Éric Pelletier, but the Quebec City bikers didn't know it. We were in the clubhouse bar along with other bikers. They gave me the addresses of both men, and I told the Quebec City bikers I'd do the contracts only after I'd completed the ones my Trois-Rivières bosses had given me. The Quebec City Angels were now better disposed toward me, and told me I should stop at the Saint-Nicolas club-house whenever I was in the area. However, Melou didn't like to see me associating with them, saying, 'You work for us!'" Quesnel's top priority was to kill Stéphane Paré. For the moment, he was watching his prey.

"It was the same routine every night. He'd leave the bar and go to sleep at his place, which wasn't far away. I'd think about my plan. At one point, I even thought about running into his Jeep with my car, then going into the bar, wearing a good disguise, and asking who owned the vehicle I'd just hit. Paré would then have followed me outside to see the damage and I'd have shot him. But all my plans failed. One day, while I was watching him, I drove into a cottage entrance to turn around and got stuck. The entrance was on a slope. I had to get help. The man on whose door I knocked was a logger. He asked me what I was doing in the area and wanted to know my name. He finally said he didn't believe me. After agreeing to pull me out with his tractor, he suggested that I not return to the area. I was anxious to get out of there. Now that a local was able to provide a good description of me, my plan fell through. I told Sudiste and the contract was put off."

There were other targets for Quesnel. His reputation was established, and the bikers wanted to make the most of him. Rick Vallée asked him to murder Robert Dubuc, president of the Saint-Jean Jokers. The unfortunate man had been foolish enough to ruffle Vallée's feathers during a meeting in a restaurant. Vallée, like every good Hells Angel, had sensitive nerves and brooked no offence.

"Dubuc was an old-timer. He'd always worked for the Angels and was fed up with being a servant, with doing all the thankless jobs. He no longer felt involved and seemed bored. He didn't even want to be on guard duty. But Dubuc was rich, and this seemed to bother some people. During his meeting with Rick, Rick asked him what he liked best: money or his colours. 'Money!' was Dubuc's reply. That's what angered and offended Rick. He was so sure he wanted him killed that, in the days that followed, he brought together the other Jokers to tell them there wouldn't be a general purge, that only Dubuc would be done in. The guys didn't ask many questions. Rick told me to be ready. Dubuc's days were numbered.

"Rick wanted to put Dubuc's nerves to the test. It happened one evening at his place, when all the members came over to give him the proceeds from the club's businesses: drugs, prostitution, and extortion. Two money-counting machines were operating almost nonstop. Dubuc was the last one to arrive. To find out whether he suspected anything, Rick asked him to go to Place Longueuil with me to get his car. I was armed and could easily have killed him that night. However, I didn't know whether he still owed Rick money, so I chose to wait. Later, I told Rick that Dubuc suspected nothing.

"That's when I learned I'd be doing the hit with Raven, one of the organization's foremost killers, a man whose talents as an assassin were internationally renowned. Rick told him about our mission when he arrived that night, and Raven seemed to agree. We chatted a little and everything appeared okay. When he left, Raven was carrying a hockey bag holding $1 million, which he was to take to one of the group's numerous hiding places. Sometimes, those places turned out to be perfectly legitimate apartments whose tenants agreed to keep packages for a while, in exchange for compensation. Usually, they wouldn't know what the bag contained. The Angels have plenty of stashes."

Murdering Robert Dubuc was now an urgent matter. In the days that followed, Quesnel stayed at the Sheraton Hotel on René Lévesque Boulevard in Montreal, waiting for Raven to arrive. Once together, Quesnel and Raven would kill Dubuc. Quesnel felt all the more important since he was getting ready to liquidate an influential man, a biker who had his colours. He was ready to do it and didn't question why Dubuc had to die. He would do what earned him the most money and respect. He would do what he was asked to do. The weapons he was given for the job were a submachine gun and a .44 magnum pistol. After spending three days in the hotel waiting for his accomplice, Quesnel finally got a message on his pager. He had to meet Rick Vallée in another hotel immediately.

"When I reached the meeting place, I saw that something serious was going on. Another Angel, Dan, was there as well. There was panic in the air. I was told that Raven had disappeared. No one had heard from him since he left Rick's place with the bag holding $1 million. Dan suggested that he might have been kidnapped by the Rock Machine. The guys were freaking out and the atmosphere was heavy. Raven was the Angel who'd killed the most people in Canada, and he was known worldwide. He was the honorary leader of the Filthy Few and the only biker allowed to wear the famous Nazi-style ss flag on motorbike rides. The guys were really worried about him. A few days later, one of Raven's friends called the clubhouse, asking that someone come to pick Raven up. He was hiding in Quebec City, suffering from a nervous breakdown. On occasion, he'd get depressed and, when he did, he wanted to give all his possessions to friends. Luckily for him, they declined. So Raven was brought back to Trois-Rivières, where the guys made sure he got proper medical treatment. He was rather quiet during that period."

Another event, which indirectly involved Raven, characterized the life Quesnel was living at the time.

"I was getting smashed, going around the bars with Jules, another Angel recruit. As was often the case, this one time we went back to the clubhouse after the bars closed. Several people were with us, and I didn't know who they were. There was this young man in particular, and I was shaking him up quite a bit, giving him orders. He obeyed and seemed scared of me. The next day, Raven told me that the young fellow who'd been with us at the clubhouse was his son. That's all he said, but I got the message."

With Raven indisposed, the murder of the Jokers' president was put off. The dust had to settle first. Quesnel, however, wasn't idle; he wasn't given time to be. When one murder failed, another was immediately planned. Quesnel was hot during this time, and the bikers wanted to make the most of it. They asked him to kill Richard Delcourt, a PCP dealer who used to work for Jacques Ferland, the man Quesnel had murdered a few weeks earlier in Grondines. The time was March 1995. Sudiste was the one to give Quesnel the contract. Nicknamed Chico, Delcourt lived in Sainte-Thècle, in the Mauricie. He owned and raised horses. The Hells Angels resented him for importing cocaine, which cut into profits from their drug trade. The thirty-eight-year-old Delcourt had to die.

"Sudiste drove with me to Sainte-Thècle, some thirty minutes from Trois-Rivières, to show me where Richard Delcourt lived. He described him, specifying that he had a scar on his nose, and told me he drove a Cherokee. Sudiste also showed me a spot, near a school, where I could get a good view of Delcourt's home, a renovated old country house. He suggested that, following the crime, I hide in a house in the neighbouring village of Montauban that belonged to a member of the Blatnois. I agreed. While driving back to Trois-Rivières, I decided to ask my buddy Pit Caron to help me kill Delcourt. It had been a while since I'd last heard from him, so I went to see him in Quebec City."

Caron wasn't sure he wanted the job Quesnel offered him. Before giving his answer, he went to Sainte-Thècle with him, to see where Delcourt lived. As they drove in front of the house, the two killers saw a man shovelling snow in the entrance. In jest, Quesnel told

Caron that he would kill Delcourt right away. "We'll shoot, then check if the guy has a scar on his nose." The comment seemed to unsettle Caron. Quesnel noticed, but said nothing. Before leaving him, Caron asked Quesnel to call him on his pager when he was ready to go into action. For the job, Quesnel stole the getaway car, a red Chrysler. Meanwhile, the Grand-Mère Blatnois were readying the house in Montauban for the killer.

"After I'd set everything up, I tried to reach Pit several times to give him the signal, but he never called me back. I was confident the contract would be easy, and I decided to act alone.

What Quesnel didn't know was that, on the day set for the murder, Caron was in the offices of the QPF in Quebec City.

"I headed to the house in Montauban to get changed. I slipped on canvas sports clothes, as well as a wig, fake glasses, a cap, and slippers. According to my plan, I wouldn't have to get out of my car and I didn't want to 'burn' my new running shoes. I brought along my .357 magnum. Driving a rented car, I went to see if the stolen Chrysler was still where I'd left it. I changed vehicles on a concession road where there was no traffic and headed to Delcourt's house. Since his sister was married to a Blatnois, I'd even been given his phone number. Once I was near his place, I called him.

" 'Hello,' a man answered.

"'Chico Delcourt?'

"'Yes, that's me. Who is it?'

"'Come outside, I'll be there in a minute. I want to talk to you about buying a horse.'

"'Okay, come on over.'

"I had a loaded pistol under my thigh and wanted Delcourt to walk up to the car so I could shoot him. But it didn't happen that way. Delcourt stayed on his porch, far enough away that I might miss him. He was wearing a bathrobe and seemed very wary.

"'You know full well I haven't come to see your horses,' I shouted out to him.

"'Yeah . . .'

"'People in Quebec City want to see you and they asked me to pick you up. Don't worry. If they wanted to kill you, they'd have done things differently.'

"'Okay, I'll fetch my things and I'll be back.'

"I was making it up. I didn't know how I'd kill him, but I knew I would. I made sure my weapon was well concealed and waited for a few seconds. I was pretty surprised that he went along with my plan so readily. He came back, climbed into the car, and we headed for Quebec City. He was nervous, didn't talk, and seemed to be hot. He rolled down his window. I broached the conversation.

"'So why do the Quebec City Angels want to see you?'

"'I don't know. This territory is controlled by the Trois-Rivières guys.'

"'Are you armed?'

"'No, even though my buddy Ferland was killed last month.'

"'Do you know why he was killed?'

"'No,' Delcourt replied, seemingly not wanting to elaborate.

"'Wasn't there a survivor in that incident?' I asked.

"'Yes.'

"'Do you think he'll be able to help the cops?'

"'I don't know.'

"As we were talking, my brain was working very hard to think of the best way to kill him. We were driving along Highway 363, a small, quiet road between Saint-Ubalde and Saint-Casimir, in the Portneuf region. I slowed the car down. I knew this was the ideal place to act, and thought about killing him in the car. But I told myself that he might have time to react before I pulled out my gun. At that point, he made a comment that helped things.

"'We won't reach Quebec City very soon at this speed,' he said.

"'I don't have a driver's licence and don't want to be stopped,' I answered.

"'I can drive, if you want.'

"'Good idea.'

"I stopped on the edge of the road, in a spot where there were no houses. I told him, 'Okay, let's trade places,' and he got out. I grabbed my weapon and climbed out as well. I pointed my revolver at his face, and I saw his fear. I don't know why, but I blurted out, 'Good night!' He only had time enough to say, 'No, not that!' then he tried to run. I took my time aiming at his back, and then I fired. He collapsed. He wasn't moving. I approached and fired another bullet into his head. Then I grabbed his legs and dragged him into the ditch, leaving him in the snow. People driving by wouldn't be able to see him. To make sure the job was done, I fired the remaining bullets into his head. I returned to the car and left."

Quesnel drove back to his car and ditched the one he'd stolen, then headed to Montauban. On the way, he tossed his weapon out the window. Once he reached the house that had been lent to him, he burned all his clothes in the fireplace. He took a shower, got rid of the ashes, and drove back to Trois-Rivières.

"I reached the clubhouse at the same time as Rick and Paulo, both of whom were full-patch members. It was 3 A.M., and Rick immediately said, 'You look happy. I'm sure you got the scumbag!' I grabbed a piece of paper and began writing down how things had happened. It was safer to tell them that way. Afterwards, I poured myself a stiff belt of Scotch, ate, and went to bed. It had been a hard day. The following morning, Melou was told that I'd fulfilled my contract. He was very happy, as were all other members of the chapter. After learning all the details of the crime, he decided to get rid of the rental car to be sure the police wouldn't find any evidence. A prospect also burned some stuff in the container located behind the clubhouse. I was proud. I'd done everything myself."

Quesnel had his moment of glory the following weekend, in Sherbrooke, at a gathering of Hells Angels from every corner of the country. Affiliated clubs also joined in the celebration, as did certain Angels from the United States. The Delta Hotel was packed with bikers. It was total bedlam. Quesnel shared his room with Fanny, a stripper from the Folichon club, who had come with him to see if she could make money table dancing. The bikers had transformed one of the hotel's huge conference rooms into a strip bar. Another room was used as a discotheque. Prostitutes and strippers were everywhere. The Hells Angels had taken total control of the hotel.

"The guys were smoking joints everywhere, in the hallways, the elevators, in the lobby. Rooms were specifically set aside for prostitutes. It was crazy, there were bikers and beautiful girls everywhere. Fanny finally decided to stay and the Nomads were continually asking her to dance for them. She danced naked, even in the hotel restaurant, the only girl allowed to do so. She danced everywhere, even in front of the staff, and made a lot of money that weekend. As for me, I was somewhat the centre of attention. Rick and Melou couldn't stop telling me that I looked good. I was chatting with all the Angels in Quebec. I felt relaxed with everyone. That's when Rick told me, 'If everybody made as much of an effort as you do, the war wouldn't last long.' The bikers treated me with great respect, and my exploits were widely talked about. What I wanted was to be part of the Nomads. The guys kept telling me they'd soon need a prospect. They'd send me messages. I could feel it coming. I was in the good graces of the Trois-Rivières chapter as well, which was to be expected, since I knew all the members.

"The weekend flew by. There were so many people present that Nachos's brother, a Trois-Rivières Angel, slept in my room on the last night. I left before the party ended. Melou was a little upset at my leaving without telling him, but I needed some breathing space. I went to Quebec City to see Sandra, a girl who danced at the Folichon. I felt a little guilty, since she was the girlfriend of my good buddy, Nose. He was in jail, and I didn't want to steal his girlfriend, but I was really attracted to her. She was a lot of fun, and sang in amateur contests. We went to some country-and-western bars, where I was sure I wouldn't run into any Angels and could consume whatever I wanted. I spent hours joking around with old men. Sandra was having a good time and doing everything to attract me. These outings were good for me, allowing me to have a little breathing space – and to release the tension."

During this period, Quesnel was consuming a lot of drugs. Mostly alcohol, but also ecstasy and hashish, as well as PCP and cocaine on the sly. The Hells Angels have frowned on cocaine since the mid-1980s. Laval's North chapter lost several members in a now-famous purge. A half-dozen bikers were killed and the Saint Lawrence River became a Hells Angels' graveyard. The victims were resented for a variety of reasons, but particularly for their unbridled consumption of cocaine.

During his bar crawl through Quebec City, Quesnel met Pit Caron. The two went for a walk along the bank of the Saint-Charles River. At first, Quesnel felt a little uncomfortable with Caron. After all, he had gone ahead with Delcourt's murder without him. He told Caron, "Don't worry, Pit, there'll be other contracts." Caron wanted to know how the murder went, and Quesnel told him everything. Afterwards, the two men shared a quick meal before heading off separately. Quesnel had to get back to Trois-Rivières. What he didn't know at the time was that his buddy had just trapped him. Caron had been turned by the police and was wearing a listening device. The date was March 28, 1995.

"Pit Caron had been talking to us since January," says Insp. Pierre Frenette. "He started very slowly, concealing many important details. At first, he didn't tell us he'd participated in Ferland's murder. Later, he started talking, and our job was to corroborate the information he gave us."

"When I got back to the Trois-Rivières clubhouse, Melou was waiting for me," Quesnel says. "He said I should have told him I was leaving the hotel, that he'd needed my services, but didn't know where I was. I didn't really believe him. I think he just wanted me to feel guilty. Even though he was a little angry, he still gave me another contract. It was to kill a Rock Machine member from Quebec City, whom I knew a little. Melou wrote his name on the blackboard and asked if I knew him. I said yes. He then wrote $15,000 on the blackboard, meaning that's how much the contract would earn me.

"'Do you have details about him?' I asked.

"'He lives near the Kentucky Fried Chicken restaurant on Charest Boulevard. Anyhow, you'll soon get the exact address. Some guys are now working on his case.'

"'Okay, I'll do the job.'

"I think Melou wanted to move the battlefield, since things had quietened down in Montreal. Whenever we killed a Rock Machine member, the others would disappear for a month. I suspect that he wanted to take over some new territory. At the time, the Quebec City Angels were having problems. The organization felt that they weren't being aggressive enough. They hadn't done anything since the war began. I think Melou wanted to teach them a lesson. For a few days, I tried to locate my target. Fat André, who hung around the Trois-Rivières Angels, knew that my target owned a red pickup. He'd told me this one evening when we'd had lots to drink. The party ended at his place, in Stoneham, where I slept on the couch.

"Rick Vallée, however, interrupted that job. Robert Dubuc's case was again on the agenda.

"'We'll knock off the Joker Dubuc together,' he said.

"'How will we do it?' I asked.

"'You take him to see a hydroponic greenhouse in Drummondville, and kill him there. I'll be in the area to pick you up.'

"I thought the plan was good. So now I had two major contracts to fulfill. Rick told me to be ready, since he might call me at any time. But he let me go back to Quebec City for the weekend. We even agreed to leave for Acapulco the following Monday.

But it was not to happen. On Saturday, April 1, 1995, Quesnel's dream of a life with the Angels came to a sudden end when the QPF stopped his car and arrested him on Sainte-Foy Boulevard in Quebec City. At first, Quesnel didn't consider being stopped by the police to be serious.

"I was sure I was being pulled over for running a Stop sign or a red light. I had nothing to worry about, since the murders I'd committed had been well carried out. However, I quickly changed my mind about the seriousness of my arrest when I saw a policeman, in an unmarked car, pointing his gun at my face. Det. Guy Lamontagne was signalling me to stop. The lights on his vehicle were flashing. So I pulled up to the edge of the road. It would've been useless for me to run away anyhow, since I wasn't armed. And things went very quickly once I'd stopped. I ended up in the middle of the road, face on the ground, a revolver pressed against my head. The police officers took me to QPF headquarters on Pierre-Bertrand Boulevard in Quebec City. They said I'd been carrying a bomb. It was an excuse. Once inside the police station, I spotted a team of detectives who were with the QPF's personal crimes division and the Montreal crime prevention squad.

"A detective offered me coffee and cigarettes, then told me that I was under arrest for the possession of explosives and that my vehicle was undergoing a thorough check. I wasn't too nervous at first. However, after a few hours, I was getting fed up with being in police custody, especially since their excuse for holding me didn't stand up. While I was being kept at QPF headquarters, other officers were searching Sandra Beaulieu's

apartment, where I'd spent the previous night. The
hours passed, and I was getting more and more irrita-
ble. At one point, I started bawling out Detective
Lamontagne, whose smile was a little too cheeky for my
liking. I told him, 'When I get out, I'll blow up three or
four cars. You'll find out what real bombs are, and we'll
see if you're still smiling then!' Lamontagne slapped me
with a new charge – uttering a death threat. I was tired
and had got carried away. The police, however, were
happy. With this new charge, they could put me in jail
until my hearing, and that's what they did. What I didn't
know at the time was that Pit was spilling his guts and
telling the whole story. He'd nearly completed his deposition. The cops also wanted to prevent me from going
to Mexico."

Detectives already knew about the plans made
by Quesnel and Vallée. They'd successfully bugged
the Trois-Rivières clubhouse some time earlier. They
knew that Quesnel and Vallée planned to kill Robert
Dubuc, then head for Mexico two days later. Frenette,
who was present at Quesnel's arrest, says, "I'd been
tailing him for some time. To me, he was a killer, an
animal. He was a target who might help us make
serious progress with Project Nordic. Obviously, we
were going after his bosses."

"So I went to court and was charged with uttering
death threats," Quesnel says.

"Then, on Sunday, April 2, late in the evening, the same detectives picked me up at the Quebec City prison, and took me back to QPF headquarters. This time, it was serious. I was charged with the murders of Richard Delcourt and Jacques Ferland.

"Detective Lamontagne piled it on: 'You'll see, this time there'll be so many charges against you that you'll spend the rest of your days in jail.' I didn't reply, negotiating instead for permission to call my lawyer, who sent me his associate. He arrived very quickly, since he'd been bowling near the police station. I rapidly explained the situation, telling him I was being charged with two murders and that other charges were likely to follow. I asked him to stay with me during the interrogation, but this wasn't allowed. When he left, he told the detectives, 'I'm warning you, my client won't talk to you. He'll tell you nothing.'"

4

CHECKMATE

DETECTIVES ARE SKILLED at getting people to talk. They study all the techniques and know every trick. By playing on the nerves of those being questioned, they try to make them crack. They understand psychology and use it to their advantage, taking the time needed to wear suspects down. This was how they acted with Serge Quesnel. No one is more stubborn than the detective who wants someone to talk.

"Bélanger was a tall cop, with grey hair. He was very experienced. He started questioning me in a small room with walls covered in beige carpeting from floor to ceiling. It was well soundproofed. Bélanger walked in and talked to me about this and that, asking about the murders, but I pretended not to know what he meant. I played innocent, in both senses of the word. But detectives are skilful at playing that little game. Once in a while, he would walk out and leave me alone. I was tired and fell asleep each time, and as soon as I did, he would come back and wake me up. He must have been using a camera to spy on me. The cops did this to me several times.

"You get completely disoriented in a room like that, and I had no idea of the time, nor even what day it was. Seated on a small wooden chair, hands tied behind my back, wedged between the wall and a wood table, I wasn't very comfortable. Detectives generally sit very close to the person being questioned, to invade the comfort space needed between two strangers. It was very unnerving. You never know whether the cop is going to slap you. Bélanger was sitting on the table, a few centimetres from me. Once in a while, he'd raise his voice. Other times, he tried to make me laugh. He told me I could still save myself, and that he was in a position to help me. He especially tried to find my weak spot, to touch my emotions. His goal was to work on my feelings till I cracked."

Quesnel's interrogation went on for many hours. Detectives took turns, trying to make him talk, but Quesnel held out. So far, he had no reason to believe that the cops had solid evidence against him. This gave him confidence. But the situation turned unexpectedly.

"Detectives Gaston Robitaille and Guy Lamontagne, 'Mr. Smiles,' arrived to relieve the other team.

Lamontagne began by telling me that, even if he were laughing, the jury would believe him, since he was pleasant, unlike me. Without giving me time to reply, he related a few important details concerning the murders, that of Jacques Ferland in particular. Accurate details. When he mentioned the famous roll of tape, I knew that Pit was cooperating with them. I suddenly realized things were serious. That's when I understood I was in deep trouble. The cops purposely piled it on. They knew I was shaken and even showed me parts of Pit's signed deposition. But since I didn't seem sufficiently shaken up, the cops decided to deal a decisive blow: they played a recording of the conversation Pit and I had had on the bank of the Saint-Charles River concerning Delcourt's murder. I was very dismayed. Pit had seemed a little strange at the time, but I never, ever, would've thought he'd go over to the police.

"I was on the ropes, but didn't want to show it. I continued to deny my role, but the cops took turns, letting me know the evidence they had that had been provided by my former accomplice. All of it was true. And throughout these disclosures, the cops would talk about the beauty of life and the possibility of making a fresh start. It was an invitation to come into their camp. They weren't crazy. They knew I was really shaken. I was face to face with myself and couldn't run away. Reality was catching up to me. I was in pain. At the same time, I understood they were offering me an opportunity to start a new life, to leave the world of crime. I realized that I no longer wanted to kill people and could no longer live with that pressure. I wanted to experience something different. Pit's statement incriminated Nachos, a full-patch member of the Trois-Rivières chapter. That was serious. The bikers considered me to be responsible for Pit and for his actions. Melou had even given me a serious warning about Pit. I was in rather deep shit. Would they put a price on my head? I was seriously wondering.

"I began to think about cooperating with the cops. I couldn't stop thinking that Pit had saved his neck this way. The idea was tempting. I was faced with a choice: I could either leave the criminal world by cooperating with the law, or stay with my accomplices. My decision was strongly influenced by the desire to find a new way of living. I realized that I wanted to see the other side of life, to give up the extreme pressure of being a criminal and a killer, even if the sentence was heavy. I didn't think there was any other solution.

"Before the media picked up the story, I phoned a few relatives to tell them about my decision. Oddly, I felt no hatred for Pit. He'd decided to save himself by co-operating, to stay alive. But I must admit I felt a twinge of sorrow at the idea of selling out the Hells Angels. They'd allowed me to experience intense emotions over the last months. My life had been filled with parties and danger. But none of that mattered any longer. I had to do what was in my best interest. I chose to cooperate and to trust the cops. Anyhow, they had a very compelling argument when they said, 'Unlike the bikers, we won't kill you!' They convinced me that I could make a fresh start and redeem myself."

QPF detectives, especially Lamontagne and Robitaille, were proud of their achievement. Not only had they captured the most active Hells Angels killer at the time, but they had just convinced him to cross over into the police camp. This was a phenomenal accomplishment, and the police celebrated. The Hells Angels organization would suffer a tremendous blow. Serge Quesnel was poised to testify against his bosses.

"After I made my decision I wanted to get some sleep, but the cops wouldn't let me. They told me I had to make a statement about Ferland's murder, to prove my good faith. I didn't have the energy to argue and did as they asked. Anyhow, I felt overtaken by events. Barely a few hours earlier, I had had goals and ambitions, and now everything had come crashing down. I gave them my statement, and was escorted back to the QPF cell-block. There was no question of my returning to the detention centre. From then on, I was under police protection. The small cell I was given had no bedding. So I went to sleep with my clothes on, covered with only a thin yellow blanket, the kind cops use to shroud corpses.

It had been forty-eight hours since my arrest, and I'd just made a very important decision. The type of decision that disrupts your life."

Quesnel's decision astonished his relatives. His parents were worried. They knew the Hells Angels' reputation. His father, who lives in the Quebec City area, grew more suspicious after his son's decision was made public.

"I was more aware of the comings and goings around me. I contacted the QPF when I noticed a biker driving near my house. I'd even jotted down his licence number. The police checked into it and told me he was a man from the Sherbrooke area who'd driven by my place purely as a coincidence. He wasn't looking for me. The police took advantage of this event to meet me at my home. They wanted to see where I lived. I told them I owned a rifle and that I wouldn't hesitate to use it if I had unexpected visitors. I must admit that I was nervous. I wasn't looking under my car, or anything like that, but I was always a little suspicious. The situation didn't prevent me from going out, from going on with my life, but I was always a little wary, even though I knew that the Hells Angels, by tradition, never attack family members. It's an unwritten rule."

The QPF was busy in the hours following Quesnel's confession. At 10:30 A.M., on April 3, some thirty police officers showed up at the entrance of the Hells Angels clubhouse on Saint-Jean Boulevard, in Trois-Rivières-Ouest. They announced their arrival on the intercom and insisted that the biker on duty in the observation room open the gate. Bikers rarely offer any resistance during this type of police operation, and the officers entered the clubhouse barely two minutes after they arrived. The four men inside were immediately arrested.

At the same time, on Cherbourg Street, near the clubhouse, other police surrounded Melou Roy and Nachos's lavish homes. Dozens of onlookers and journalists from the Mauricie area witnessed the operation. Six people were arrested, including Nachos and Roy. Police didn't say anything about their motives for the arrests. They insisted that the journalists stick to the facts. The news was a very hot topic. A lawyer for the bikers, Roger Bellemare, willingly gave interviews to the media to denounce certain police practices. The bikers arrested in the clubhouse were taken outside and were forced to lie down, their faces pressed against the ground, for more than an hour. Bellemare was not allowed to talk to his clients, and claimed that police were flouting the Canadian Charter of Rights and Freedoms.

The police offensive wasn't over. It continued the next day in Quebec City, when several houses were taken by storm. More arrests were made. Then, on April 6, very early in the morning, QPF officers went to the

Blatnois clubhouse, in Grand-Mère. Some thirty police officers showed up and emptied the premises. Three bikers were arrested, making a total of sixteen arrests for this operation. It was also during this raid that the QPF first admitted to having information from Serge Quesnel and Michel Caron.

"It was a rude awakening. The raids were the only thing newspapers were talking about, and I was shaken. All the media knew about it. Melou had been arrested, along with Rick Vallée, Sudiste, and Nachos. The cops had also nabbed Mario, Clermont, and Richard from the affiliated clubs. I felt things had gone really quickly. The detectives were jumping for joy. I was beginning to realize how important a catch I was. Lamontagne and Robitaille even asked me if I would agree to cooperate only with them, likely because they wanted to see the case through to the end. After all, they were the ones who had made me switch sides. The two detectives would certainly be doing a lot of overtime as I had lots to say. I agreed. After all, the two of them knew me a little better than the others did. They were saying that if any investigators arrived from Montreal, I should tell them that I preferred working with the two Quebec City detectives. I agreed, and put myself in their hands. But at that point I still didn't understand all the consequences of my decision. I had had practically no time to think. All I had done was answer questions. I was finally placed in the QPF's Quebec City headquarters, where I would stay while cooperating with the police, and gradually understood that I was in a good position to take a little advantage of the situation. Someone in authority gave me permission to choose the paint colours for the wing I'd be living in, so I chose white and grey."

Insp. Pierre Frenette says that the killer-informant benefited from a combination of circumstances. Several reasons led to his being placed in the QPF's Quebec City headquarters.

"Serge Quesnel was detained there because there was no other place for him at first. The cellblock where we jailed him hadn't been used for years. It was totally decrepit, so we refurbished the wing. I found barbells at the provincial police academy in Nicolet, and a fridge was brought in. We felt this was the safest place to keep him. At that time, we couldn't imagine sending him to jail. We'd taken him to a detention centre, and the administrators there were so afraid of an armed attack that they placed a tow truck in front of the entrance to prevent anyone from seeing what would be going on inside when Quesnel arrived."

The informant was imprisoned inside QPF headquarters, where the police officers responsible for watching over him bent over backwards to make his life pleasant. However, despite this royal treatment, Quesnel didn't feel good at all.

"The first days weren't easy. It was strange to live with cops all the time. On one of the first mornings I woke up at QPF headquarters, I was surprised to see four moustached cops seated in front of my TV, looking like four guards in Saddam Hussein's army. Quite a change from the bikers I'd seen when I woke up at the Trois-Rivières clubhouse. But the cops tried to make my life easy. The fifteen officers in charge of guarding me were decent. I had a problem with the uniform, but for the rest, the guys were mostly very nice.

"One morning, I saw my face on the front page of a newspaper with the title 'informant.' I found this hard to take. I couldn't get used to being identified as an informant. Yet, that's what I'd become. During this time, I asked to see a psychologist, since I was suffering from anxiety and depression. The detectives called a woman who happened to have some QPF officers among her patients. She refused to meet me, and for good reason. She was the sister of Richard Jobin, the first man I killed in 1993. But she behaved like a true professional. She probably hated me too much to help me, but she could have driven me to commit suicide, since I was so fragile at the time. Instead, she told the detective that she was the sister of one of my victims. I thank her for this, and apologize for bringing pain to her and to her family."

The families of Quesnel's victims weren't the only ones suffering. His family did, as well. When they learned that he was being charged with five murders, several assaults, and conspiracies to commit murder, Quesnel's parents were stunned. His father still has trouble merely recalling the facts.

"I knew that you had to commit crimes to join the bikers. I also knew that my boy was no saint, but when I heard that he'd killed five people. When we saw each other again after his arrest, following a five-year separation, the first thing I told Serge was that I could never accept what he'd done. I disagree with the motives behind those crimes. I told him that I didn't want to hear about them and that I'd never talk to him about them again. And I haven't."

At first, Quesnel's father thought that his son had become an informant because he had no other choice.

"Serge became an informant out of obligation. It was his only way out. The first time I visited him at the police station in Quebec City, I saw no willingness in my son to cooperate with the police in any way. On the contrary. He asked the police officer guarding him to leave us alone. The officer refused, and Serge told him to go to hell. At that point, I really couldn't imagine he'd end up on the police side."

"There were several police officers who didn't believe in Serge Quesnel," says Frenette. "His behaviour didn't inspire anyone's confidence. Some of my colleagues were certain that he would change his mind along the way. They seriously doubted his potential and trusted Pit Caron a lot more. They didn't think Quesnel was very bright. At first, even after agreeing to cooperate with us, Quesnel was pretty lazy. He wanted to do things his way and according to his whims. Criminals are often like that. They're used to easy living, and getting what they want, when they want it."

For Quesnel, the days started to resemble one another. He answered questions from detectives, repeated his version of the facts, and reiterated the details of a plot, fight, or murder. He talked about the adventure of life in Hells Angels country. The detectives were gloating. They had been wanting to arrest Melou Roy and Rick Vallée, two of the big names on the Quebec crime scene, for a long time, and they had finally succeeded. The new informant's confessions were dynamite. The facts he gave them were reasonably accurate, and they were confident about the upcoming trials. Quesnel was likely the biggest fish they had caught among the bikers in a long time. He was close to the leaders, and his fall could bring down several more people. The police and prosecutors took full advantage of the situation. No effort was spared to ensure that the star informant was comfortably set up, so that he could rest thoroughly and recall events more precisely.

Serge Quesnel enjoyed those early months in detention.

"I was really well treated at the QPF station. The detectives did everything to ensure my comfort. A corner had even been set up with a gym where I could train. And then, imagine, Pit Caron, the very man who denounced me to the cops, was brought to join me. Contrary to what some might think, I didn't hold the fact he'd become an informant against him. I understood what he'd done. Four cops were guarding us. We couldn't talk about the upcoming trials, but we talked about other things.

"We were given first-class treatment. It seemed as though the QPF had an unlimited budget for several months and we got everything we asked for. Pit and I were trying to spend as much money as possible. I really liked good Cuban cigars, especially Montecristos and Cohibas. A single one of those cigars costs between $30 and $50, and I only had to ask for them. A cop would take money out of the small blue box, then hop into an unmarked car and rush off to the Tremblay tobacconist, which was renowned for its cigars. I treated myself. A man came to clean our cells every day. The state also took care of getting us haircuts. Once in a while the cops refused requests that were too costly, when Pit and I were exaggerating. But, more often than not, they gave us what we asked for. Our clothes were sent to the cleaners and came back well pressed and on hangers. I often took advantage of the situation and spoiled my visitors. It was easy.

"That's when I found out that the police's priority was to get me to sign a contract. They needed me to testify in court, and high-ranking QPF officers were ready to give a lot to get me to accept. But I wasn't stupid, I could see their game. I knew that my testimonies were worth a lot. The way I was being treated was proof of that."

"At first, Quesnel was spoiled by the officers taking care of him," admits Frenette. "Besides, the guys guarding him were buying peace in a way by doing nearly everything he asked. Quesnel had a certain power. If one of the police guards didn't suit him, he'd bellyache so much that the officer would be sent away. The others preferred to give him what he wanted, rather than hearing his continual complaints."

And Quesnel has quite a temper. The interrogations done by the various detectives didn't always go smoothly. He didn't get on with every officer, and sparks sometimes flew. He even asked that certain cops no longer be allowed to work with him. He had been dealt a good hand and took advantage of it. But he also did a lot of thinking, going over everything that happened before and since his arrest. The first conversations with detectives; the discovery of an informant – in this case, his friend Pit; the chronology of events. There's one detail that haunts him – the QPF knew that Richard Delcourt would be killed, but hadn't intervened to stop it.

"The QPF didn't do its job. Pit was already collaborating with the police and had told them about my offer to involve him in Chico Delcourt's murder, so the cops were aware of my intention. They knew that Delcourt was in danger and did nothing to protect him. Perhaps I was quicker than the cops on that occasion. But, I have trouble understanding the QPF's attitude in the Delcourt affair. In the days before the crime, detectives even accompanied Pit to Delcourt's house in Sainte-Thècle, to see where the murder would take place. Someone, somewhere, didn't do his job."

Criminals in the situation Quesnel was in are called repentant witnesses, a label that goes over better with jurors. Quesnel knew that the government wanted him to sign the informant contract, and that it was ready to pay big money to nab his bosses. So detectives let him set the pace of their investigation. With the amount of information he was in a position to disclose, they knew better than to rush him. So they spared no effort to ensure that he was in a frame of mind conducive to recalling all details. To gather as much information as possible, they took a helicopter to visit the places in the Upper Mauricie where each of the murders had been committed. Quesnel always went along for the ride. During the summer, he and his guards went everywhere. They drove all the roads that Quesnel had taken in the five months he spent with the Hells Angels. And he had covered a lot of ground, enough to have found a mechanic in Shawinigan who had agreed to tamper with the odometers of the vehicles he rented so that he could save money.

Quesnel enjoyed his outings with the police. It was good for him to leave his cell and get some fresh air. He particularly enjoyed the helicopter rides.

"I really liked to travel in a helicopter. Seeing nature from high up in the air was really great. At one point, I thought about committing suicide by jumping out of the helicopter. That would've set tongues wagging. Imagine the headline: 'PRISONER JUMPS OFF QPF HELICOPTER.' But I lacked the courage. It was better to cooperate. It was a lot of work, because I had to remember everything. Detectives followed me everywhere, taking notes and asking questions. Most of them weren't excessively forceful; they didn't put too much pressure on me. If one day's schedule was heavy, the next day would be more mellow. At times, I felt more important than the premier, since I toured Quebec with more bodyguards than he did. We'd eat at a restaurant, and return to the police station at day's end.

"One day, while we were at a restaurant in Nicolet, the waitress at our table kept staring at me, saying, 'I think I know you.' I told her that she must be mistaken. But she insisted, asking whether I was in a soap opera. The detectives had had enough. They couldn't afford to take the least risk. So one of them asked that everything we had ordered be wrapped so we could take it with us. He paid the bill and we left.

"Those days broke up the monotony of my detention. I really loved them. I had the trust of the officers accompanying me. I could have escaped several times. The police really believed in my willingness to make a fresh start. We covered a lot of ground, going to Montreal to visit the hotels where I'd hatched various plots with my former 'partners.' We'd gone to nearly all the large hotels in the city. Often, there were people there who remembered us. Those hotels have security systems that allow them to communicate and exchange information with the police. For example, the head of security at the Meridien remembered Rick, Melou, and me. He had a good reason to. One of us had left a 9 mm pistol in the drawer of a bedside table. The woman in charge of security at the InterContinental Hotel also remembered us. We'd been filmed, pretending not to know each other, before holding a meeting in one of the rooms. The videotape, now in police hands, showed me standing beside the wife of an Arab sheik who'd rented an entire floor. I was holding a sports bag filled with weapons and dynamite. Imagine if it had exploded!

"Those visits changed my routine. One day, our vehicle broke down on Saint Catherine Street. Since this isn't a neighbourhood where the cops are particularly liked, and since more and more people were giving us funny looks, it wasn't long before another vehicle arrived to take us to Parthenais station. While travelling, especially from Quebec City to Montreal, I'd often sit next to the driver, and I'd be the one who'd turn on the flashing lights and the siren to move the vehicles ahead of us out of the way. I was beginning to be on friendly terms with some detectives. They trusted me more and more."

"Quesnel certainly liked to come along with us to the scenes of his crimes," says Frenette. "All inmates like to do this. To them, it's much better than staying in jail. It breaks their routine."

Quesnel says, "I'd go into the offices of detectives who specialized in fighting biker gangs, and often spotted objects that had belonged to the Hells Angels, for example, stickers that only full-patch members are allowed to own. In biker clubhouses, objects bearing the Angels logo are kept under lock and key. Chapter secretaries are responsible for them. The detective displayed these objects as though they were hunting trophies. One of these policemen even promised me a Hells Angels flag, like the ones that fly over clubhouses all over the world. He told me, 'I'll give it to you once you're finished testifying.'"

Quesnel told the police everything. He hid nothing. He told them all the names, all the details of the crimes he was involved in. He and the cops frequently talked about a future agreement to pay for his services as an informant. But the actual agreement did not concern the police. Quesnel would meet with the committee responsible for negotiating agreements with informants once he had related everything about his life as a criminal. He had resolved to try to get as much as possible out of the deal. In the meantime, he cooperated, though police had to prod him at times to make more of an effort. One day, American police officers came to Quebec City to question him about a murder committed in the United States. Rick Vallée was suspected of killing a Drug Enforcement Agency informant a few years earlier.

"I told them to get lost. After all, I didn't want Rick to get the death penalty. I wanted to concentrate on events that had taken place in Quebec. I was also getting ready to meet the committee and had even drawn up a list of demands. And they weren't minor. I wanted a million dollars, a new identity, a furnished house, a car, and so on. I also wanted my tattoos removed. I was laying it on. I knew that the organization I was denouncing was highly coveted. There weren't too many of us testifying against the Hells Angels."

Just before he was scheduled to meet this committee, Quesnel learned that he would be transferred to another QPF station. Reasons for the move remain unclear. Quesnel, however, now thinks he knows what was behind it.

"I stayed there for two weeks, dealing with new police officers and detectives. The conditions of my detention were totally unlike those I'd experienced at the QPF station on Pierre Bertrand Boulevard. I was in a strange position, and certainly didn't have the same comforts I'd known in my other cell. I suspect everything had been well planned in high places. I was nervous and worried about my future. I was anxious to meet the committee and set the terms for my being an informant. The reason for the transfer, in my opinion, was that the police wanted to destabilize me, to make sure I'd sign the agreement they'd offer. In the end, I was moved back to my quarters on Pierre-Bertrand Boulevard."

The interrogations continued. Following two months of discussions, of arguments at times, Quesnel finally met with the committee in charge of setting the terms of his informant's contract.

"My list was ready. I knew my demands were excessive, but this didn't prevent me from presenting them to the committee. Its members were Jean-Pierre Duchaine from the QPF, Yvon Houle and Arthur Fauteux from the Public Security Department, and Louise Villemure, a

lawyer representing the Attorney General. When the
meeting took place, I looked at the committee members,
pulled out my list, and put it on the table. I asked the
committee to examine my requests and left. While I was
waiting for the committee to respond, the two cops
guarding me made me promise to remain calm and not
get carried away. Then I went back before the committee. I sat at the end of the conference table, with the two
cops on either side of me. Jean-Pierre Duchaine from the
QPF spoke first. 'Your requests are excessive,' he told me,
adding, 'The first item to settle is your sentence. We
suggest a fifteen-year term.' I asked for permission to
leave the room so I could think about it. In fact, I didn't
think about it very long, since I thought it was great. I
told myself I'd serve one-sixth of that sentence and
would be released following two or three years in prison.
I was ready to accept.

"When I returned to the committee room, I got a
cold shower. Before letting me say a word, Jean-Pierre
Duchaine said he'd made a mistake, that what he'd
meant to offer was a life sentence with possibility of
parole after fifteen years. I was in shock. My blood pressure rose. I began to argue. Then Villemure, the lawyer,
intervened. She said, 'You know you're being charged
with five premeditated murders. Removing premedita-
tion is a big deal.' She then continued to talk while leafing

through the penal code. That's when I blew a fuse, telling her she was crazy and swearing. The two cops accompanying me thought this was funny. I feel sorry for losing my temper, because Villemure was very respectful. Jean-Pierre Duchaine asked me to calm down, and we continued to negotiate. Finally, we settled on a life sentence with parole after twelve years.

"Then we talked about money. They referred to it as 'living expenses,' and we reached an agreement rather quickly. I'd get $500 a week for the duration of my sentence and for three years following my release. The money would be non-taxable. The total agreement came to $390,000. As Jean-Pierre Duchaine pointed out, this was equivalent to the pay I'd get for thirty-nine murders. The amount may seem considerable, but I could have got more. I didn't try to increase it. A few months later, Yvon Houle, from the Public Security Department, disclosed that he had had permission to go up to $600 a week, which, in the end, would have amounted to nearly $80,000 more. But at the time of negotiations, I was sure I could manage the money I'd be given. By investing, for example.

"Once the issue of money was settled, I asked for and got agreement that the tattoos on my arms and the tears on my face would be removed. On my release in 2007, I'd also be given a safe place to stay, with furniture and all necessities. When the negotiations ended, I was satisfied. But I wasn't jumping for joy. I still had twelve years to serve."

"I wish he'd taken a lawyer to represent him before the committee," says Quesnel's father. "That's what I advised him to do, but he refused, telling me he was able to settle everything himself. I even offered to go with him, if only to give him my opinion of the offer he'd be given, but again he refused. He wanted to settle things his way. The contract he signed with the government, regardless of what the public thinks, isn't a large one. Listen, $500 a week to put your life on the line; $500 a week to spare the police months of investigation, which might have led nowhere? Of course, Serge did commit those crimes, but he's paying for them. The sentence he's serving has nothing to do with the money he's getting. It's to pay his debt to society."

"Many police officers were angry when they learned that Quesnel would get that much money," says Pierre Frenette. "My colleagues don't like it when crooks get paid. But the cash has to be put in perspective. Serge Quesnel gets $26,000 a year. That's not very much for the work he spared us. It all depends on how you explain his payment. Of course, $500 a week for fifteen years seems like a lot of money. But, informant contracts have existed throughout history. In the past, when the death penalty still applied, the law spared the lives of certain individuals in exchange for their cooperation. A life is worth more than $26,000."

Six days after signing the contract, on June 20, Serge Quesnel was taken to the Quebec City courthouse. There was no fanfare. He pleaded guilty to multiple charges: five unpremeditated murders, thirteen conspiracies, two assaults causing bodily harm, possession and use of a restricted weapon, and stealing a car. On the Crown attorney's recommendation, Quesnel was immediately given a life sentence with the possibility of parole after twelve years.

"I was in a strange state during my appearance and allowed myself to be carried by the events. It was really serious. I was pleading guilty to a multitude of charges. I was selling the bikers out. It was a confusing period. I preferred to roll with the punches. Things went very quickly. At the same time, perhaps to dispel my nervousness, I was making jokes. When the judge told me I could no longer own weapons following my release, I asked him if this included crossbows."

"From the moment he signed his agreement with the authorities," his father says, "Serge started cooperating completely. There are no half-measures where he's concerned. He suddenly began revealing all he knew. This worried me a little. I advised him to be careful, telling him that the authorities would let him down when he finished testifying. He wasn't being wary because he was being well treated. What with the cigars and the food, he was living the good life, for a prisoner. I'd visit him at the police station and we'd have dinner together. I thought this was rather strange, although I knew full well this was a police strategy. He was given nearly everything he wanted so that he'd cooperate as much as possible. I told him to be careful, but he didn't see things as I did."

Quesnel was sentenced one week after Pit Caron got his sentence. Thirty years of age (five years older than Quesnel), Caron received eleven years in jail for manslaughter. After the sentencing, Pierre Frenette appeared on the scene as Quesnel's handler. His job was to take care of the informer, videotape all his statements, and get him ready for the trials of the Angels he had betrayed. Not an easy task.

"At first, he treated the police as his servants," Frenette says. "He wanted us to do what he asked exactly when he asked for it. He'd call me on my pager, wanting me to drop everything to take care of his requests. We had to make it clear to him that we had activities and families outside of work; that he wasn't the only one around."

It took Quesnel a little while to get used to his two handlers, Frenette and Tony Cannavino. The latter, sometimes exasperated with Quesnel's careless attitude, had a few serious rows with him. But things finally calmed down. During this time, Quesnel was visited now and again by his mistress, Sandra Beaulieu.

"Her visits were special. The cops would pick her up two or three times a week. She'd bring me PCP by smuggling it in her vagina. Sandra would have dinner with me whenever she came over, and the bills got a little high on a few occasions. For instance, we had a bottle of wine with our meal on my birthday, and lived it up for a few hours. Sandra was still seeing Nose at Donnacona, something neither the cops nor I knew about at the time. I'm sure that Nose must have asked her questions about me. As it happened, Nose's sisters were Sandra's best friends. One day, I called Sandra's home and Nathalie, one of Nose's sisters, answered. Everyone found out very quickly that Sandra was in touch with me."

All this time, Quesnel's enemies were plotting against him. Since he was scheduled to testify against all his old friends, and had lots to say, they felt that something had to be done. They couldn't attack him physically, so they took on his credibility.

"One day, Sandra came to see me with a camera. She said she wanted souvenirs of us together. So one of the cops guarding me agreed to snap a shot of us. Sandra was in her underwear on the desk in front of me. And the pose was rather suggestive. In another photo, she was sitting on me. At that point, I was far from suspecting what was around the corner."

On July 31, the newspaper *Le Soleil* published the photo of Quesnel and his mistress on the front page. It was a bombshell. In the accompanying story, Sandra Beaulieu admitted to smuggling PCP to Quesnel. She said she had hidden the drug in her vagina. All the other media jumped on the story. Quesnel's former lawyer sent the photo to the paper, as a means of undermining Quesnel, who was scheduled to start testifying in a few days. The lawyer publicly attacked Quesnel and the QPF. In his opinion, Quesnel had made false accusations against him by saying that he'd asked him to kill an inmate called Roger Aubin. The lawyer also accused the police of having put his life in danger by telling Aubin about this presumed plot. Not satisfied with this media stunt, he even wrote to the Public Security Minister to demand protection. Quesnel was not only back in the headlines, he was also charged with conspiracy and possession of PCP. Sandra Beaulieu was also charged, as was her supplier, Rénald Laperrière.

"There was a great outcry among the public, and in QPF offices, over this story. The police force was deeply embarrassed. For my part, I pleaded guilty to the charges laid against me. I wasn't afraid that my informant's contract would be broken, since the crimes I was charged with had been committed before its official signature. Nonetheless, the judge ordered that proceedings against me be halted. I was very surprised, and so was the public.

All the more so considering that I'd pleaded guilty. Judge Michel Babin explained that simply purchasing narcotics wasn't a criminal offence."

The ruling astonished everyone. Quesnel's former lawyer, the one who was trying to discredit him, said he was outraged and claimed that Sandra Beaulieu's statement was clear enough to convict Quesnel. The young woman and her supplier didn't receive the same leniency from the court. The twenty-one-year-old stripper was given a $3,000 fine and a two-year probation. Laperrière, for his part, was sentenced to eighteen months in jail and a three-year probation.

"I never saw Sandra Beaulieu again," Quesnel says. "It's better that way. I know the lawyer took advantage of her gullibility. Following this business with the photos, she was afraid – of me, the Angels, everyone. I think she had wanted to play in the big leagues and then regretted it."

"All things considered, I don't think this was a major scandal," says Pierre Frenette. "It was only a scheme by Quesnel's former lawyer. He got his kicks out of it, but it had nothing to do with killing people. As for the drugs, someone played a trick on us. Sometimes, you don't have a choice, you have to trust people. In that case, we were had. It happens."

Quesnel went back to enjoying some good times at QPF headquarters, where he was being held.

"I was comfortable there. My quarters were something like a presidential suite. Most of the cops were decent. I was taking it easy. When the weather was nice, I'd go outside wearing Bermuda shorts and no shirt. This bothered the senior officers, especially during the week when everyone was working. I didn't care. They often asked me to get dressed, but in the summer, when it was thirty degrees Celsius, I'd still take off my T-shirt. Some secretaries were jealous because I had a table and parasol, something they'd requested for their breaks, but which had been refused. They'd say, 'Do you have to kill someone to get a parasol?' I understood their frustration. I'd have really enjoyed having some of them come over to sit with me, but the cops were doing everything to protect their witness. They didn't like my talking to just anybody. One day, while I was talking to a Quebec City journalist, a cop interrupted the conversation by ripping the phone wire out of the wall. He made it clear that I was not to talk to any journalists.

"I kept busy as best I could. One day, the detectives came to see me with a $2,000 phone bill. To pass the time, I'd been calling a girl whose number I'd got from the want ads. She had a wonderful French accent. I knew it was a sex phone line and that you had to pay, but I didn't know where I was calling. At one point, the woman asked me where I lived, and I told her, 'Quebec.' I was surprised when she said, 'Where's that?' So I asked her where she was. I was really dismayed when she said, 'Switzerland.' I immediately hung up and never called her back. The cops wanted me to pay the $2,000 phone bill, but I refused. I assume they decided to pay it for me, since they never mentioned it again."

Quesnel got along with most of the police officers around him, but, one day, he argued with one of them. He didn't like the officer's continual boasting about giving out more fines than any of his colleagues.

"We had an altercation in the afternoon. Then I decided to avenge myself that night. I waited for the cop to fall asleep, then turned on my stereo with the volume cranked up to the maximum. He seemed so shaken that I thought he'd have a heart attack. I was laughing my head off and happy to have played this trick on him. But he was furious. Some of his colleagues spoke to him, but his attitude toward me didn't change. He was eventually transferred to another department."

While all these scandals, power games, and backroom deals were happening, Quesnel was getting ready to take the big step, the one that would take him to the court where he would testify against his old friends and bosses. Quesnel wasn't anxious to take this step, not because he lacked confidence or was unsure of his testimony, but because he knew that the Hells Angels wouldn't take his betrayal sitting down. Quesnel was convinced he'd be facing the best defence lawyers in the province. Hiring the most talented and expensive lawyers is a biker trademark. He would also be facing his former friends, glowering at him with disgust across the courtroom. He knew that he could count on support from the policemen who were helping him to get ready for the trial, but he was also fully aware that on the other side, defence lawyers were carefully examining each fragment of a statement or suggestion he had made. They would walk into the courtroom well prepared and determined to get him. He knew all this. The idea of facing his former lawyer especially provoked him. Quesnel had only one desire: to make that lawyer lose face. For his own personal pleasure.

In early August, the legal apparatus was set in motion. Proceedings began in Montreal with the preliminary inquiry for Mario Lussier, Quesnel's accomplice in the murder of Claude "le Pic" Rivard. The war of words began immediately, when Crown attorney François Legault petitioned the judge to have Lussier's lawyer removed, since he was Quesnel's former lawyer, the one who introduced him to Melou Roy, president of the Angels.

"I was brought to the witness box. Lussier looked at me and, reluctantly, asked me, 'Why?' He didn't understand why I was testifying against him. I felt I was finally getting a chance to confront my former lawyer. I was sworn in and now facing Judge Céline Lamontagne. I said that Lussier's lawyer had represented me in at least four major cases. I was confident and could see I was making a good impression. I was properly dressed, wearing a jacket and beige shirt. Once I'd finished testifying, Lussier's lawyer didn't protest. I'd just won my first battle. He was declared unfit to represent the biker. He went to sit with the audience. An older man called Léo-René Maranda took over. He's one of the most famous criminal lawyers in the country."

Léo-René Maranda has a solid reputation as a lawyer, having represented, in several major cases, the Hells Angels, members of the Dubois Clan, as well as members of the Colombian Connection. He has the reputation of being a sly fox. Maranda is somewhat pretentious, and gives no quarter when facing a witness. Hearing him plead a case is a delight; facing him is a nightmare. Quesnel would discover this months later at the onset of Lussier's trial. But first, Quesnel had to face another of his former friends, Rick Vallée. The biker's preliminary inquiry began in Montreal in September. Once again, Quesnel's former lawyer was in court, representing Vallée, and Crown attorney François Legault again tried to have him declared unfit to plead the case. This time, however, the lawyer defended himself, and the court allowed him to represent the biker. Proceedings were then deferred.

They resumed in Quebec City at the end of September, when the preliminary inquiries concerning

Melou Roy and Sudiste got underway. There was much excitement in the courtroom. There were nearly as many journalists as onlookers, and the special constables in charge of courthouse security were on high alert. Many police officers were also present. The security of the premises was being taken very seriously. Once again, the Crown attorney, Alain Guimond, tried to strike a major blow, since Melou was also being represented by Quesnel's former lawyer. Guimond successfully argued his case against the lawyer, and the judge ruled that he must stand down. The lawyer was furious and decided to appeal the ruling. Meanwhile, Sudiste was being defended by Jacques Larochelle, who is peerless in his use of legal language. Two months after the start of the preliminary inquiry, the Superior Court ruled that Roy's lawyer would be able to represent him.

By now it was the end of 1995, and Serge Quesnel had a few weeks of holidays. The first trial, the one concerning Rick Vallée, did not start until March. Vallée had been charged with conspiracy to kill Robert Dubuc, the president of the Saint-Jean Jokers. Judge Jerry Zigman would hear the case.

Quesnel says, "Of course, I was feeling a lot of pressure. It seemed that the upcoming trial was all that the media were talking about. But the idea of facing my former lawyer, the one who'd put me in touch with the Angels, just motivated me even more. Frankly, whether or not Melou and the others were sentenced, my situation wouldn't change much. I tried to avoid listening to the news, since I felt I was being portrayed as a crook and slimebag. Whenever I was in the courtroom, before the public, I tried to project an image of confidence. I'd smile and was even a little cheeky at times. But this was only a mask, a shield. Whenever my eyes met Rick's, I felt all the scorn he had for me. I was ashamed. No one wants to be branded as an informant. I felt dirty."

The proceeding dragged on. Since the lawyers were debating a multitude of petitions, jurors would not be called until the beginning of September. Meanwhile, a bailiff visited Quesnel to let him know that Michel "Coriace" Landry, an inmate he assaulted at Donnacona three years earlier, was suing him for $200,000, including $100,000 in exemplary damages. Landry's lawyer was Jean-René Maranda, the son of Léo-René, who was defending Rick Vallée. Everything seemed to have been brilliantly orchestrated to unsettle Quesnel. And he was getting nervous. The authorities feared he'd lose his concentration and did all they could to reassure him. A bureaucrat with the Public Security Department promised that a clause would be added to his contract guaranteeing that the ministry would take care of all proceedings against him. Quesnel would never have to pay for anything out of his own pocket. Besides Quesnel and the bureaucrat, Capt. Marc Desprès from the QPF,

Pierre Frenette, and Tony Cannavino were at that meeting. The agreement reassured Quesnel. However, several months later, the bureaucrat went back on his word, leaving Quesnel worried that he'd have to pay. Frenette and Cannavino came to his rescue by signing a sworn statement confirming the promise made. In the end, the Quebec government would pay the bill.

Frenette says, "We signed those statements because Quesnel's lawyer, Cecil Posman, asked us to. It was the plain truth. This is done regularly in civil actions. You sign a sworn statement and avoid having to testify. Some people had promised things to Quesnel, and those promises had to be kept."

Meanwhile, at the Montreal courthouse, jury members were being chosen. Seven men and five women were eventually selected. A dramatic turn of events occurred when these jurors entered the courtroom for the first time: one of them – a woman – was challenged after telling the court that the son of her husband's cousin was a member of the Rock Machine. The trial had to go forward with only eleven jurors.

"The system is poorly designed," claim the two policemen. "Jurors are ordinary, honest human beings who are completely removed from the underworld. They're parachuted into a world that's unknown, impressive, and intimidating. They have to deal with their own emotions while they are listening to the details of sordid crimes. Having to judge bikers isn't easy, especially when they're in front of you, looking at you, and when dozens of their supporters are in the courtroom. It's not easy for the man or woman to say, 'Guilty.' I'm convinced that the system benefits the defendant."

Meanwhile Quesnel was getting ready to face the defence lawyers, whose mandate was to do all they could to get an acquittal. He would be questioned about everything. Frenette and Cannavino jogged his memory.

"I was getting ready by rereading my statements and the stenographic notes. Pierre Frenette and Tony Cannavino helped by asking me certain questions. When I made a mistake about a trivial detail, they'd tell me to think it over. This preparation went on without pressure. I totally agreed with the way these cops were doing things. Whenever my memory failed, they'd say, 'If this happens in court, you can always ask to reread your statements. At the very worst, if you forget a detail completely, say you don't remember. The important thing is to tell the truth.'"

And the moment of truth had arrived. Serge Quesnel was finally called as a witness.

"All I knew about Maranda, my adversary, was that he was one of the most expensive and best lawyers in Quebec, and that he was in his sixties. I had no idea he was so skilful and tenacious. He'd always begin his cross-examination by saying, 'Hello, Mr. Quesnel,' and then gradually move on to his questions. The first day I was in the witness box, he showed me a photo and asked, 'Do you recognize this man?' I glanced at the photo and said that I didn't. Maranda burst out laughing and said, 'Look at this photograph carefully. . . . It's you!' I was so nervous, I was completely at a loss. Whenever I was put in an embarrassing situation, he'd look at the crowd and laugh. This really got on my nerves and hurt my confidence. This was the first time in my life I'd faced a jury. It was impressive. Maranda had decided to make me suffer. He asked me to relate in front of everybody all the atrocities I'd committed in my life. He'd emphasize the worst crimes and ask me to disclose every detail. He was continually on the attack. I was completely trapped and had the impression I was on trial. By comparison, he treated his client, Rick Vallée, as a saint. It was a disconcerting cross-examination. From one question to the next, I didn't know what to do. Maranda had me in his clutches and there was no way he'd let go. If I forgot a detail, he'd bring it to the fore. He'd pick out the smallest inconsistency. I was getting more and more nervous facing this old pro, and I made mistakes. He'd take advantage of them. I could see that his game was to make me lose face in the eyes of the jury. Since this was the first in a series of trials involving the bikers, he wanted to explore my recollections as much as possible.

It would prove useful for the other trials. In short, he wouldn't let up."

During the trial, Quesnel established a record by being cross-examined for twenty-eight days in a row. Maranda questioned him for seventy hours. The former Hells Angels killer considers this trial to be one of the worst experiences of his life. The old lawyer was giving him a rough ride. By speaking softly and using his kindly grandfather's demeanour, he managed to unsettle Quesnel. And would then pillory him.

"He cross-examined me on the fifty-two statements I'd made to the police, asking me to tell the jury about plots to kill the Pelletier brothers, and then to name the members of the Gang de l'Est. Which I did. Maranda then whispered something into his assistant's ear, and the woman left the courtroom. The cross-examination went on, and then Maranda asked me to turn toward the audience and tell him if I recognized any people. Right away I spotted members of the Gang de l'Est. I was really surprised. Triumphantly, Maranda blurted out: 'Are these the people you were supposed to kill?' I answered that they were. I couldn't believe it. Richard Pelletier and 'Pep' Simard were sitting beside Hells Angels, enemies sitting side by side! Everything had been really well orchestrated. I looked really bright."

Day after day, Quesnel's nightmare continued. He was anxious, tired, and desperate to keep his head above water, but it was becoming more difficult. Quesnel now had only one goal, and that was to end his torment as soon as possible. But Rick Vallée's lawyer had absolutely no intention of letting up.

"Maranda was very well prepared. One day, he asked me to list all the names underworld people use to describe guys like me, informants. I gave him a few, but he insisted. He wanted to hear them all. I mentioned rats and stool pigeons and still the lawyer wanted more. So I finally listed all the words I could think of. Maranda then asked me to listen to an excerpt from a conversation I'd had with Pit Caron. I heard myself telling Caron, 'Sniffing coke once in a while doesn't make us rats.' Of course, Maranda wouldn't let such a wonderful opportunity slip past. He said to me, 'So, you're not rats?' And he then started to laugh. He was doing his one-man show."

Quesnel was at the end of his tether. He didn't give a damn about the trial's outcome. All he wanted was for it to end as soon as possible – or to be able to get vengeance.

"The American authorities came back to see me at QPF headquarters on Parthenais Street in Montreal. There were three of them, and they wanted to know about the murder of a man called Lee Carter. The torture I was going through during Vallée's trial convinced me to co-operate with them. It was a kind of vengeance on my part. I told them what I knew about Carter's death. They asked whether I'd agree to testify in the case, and I said I would since I didn't give a damn about Vallée's fate."

"During that trial, I saw Quesnel get discouraged a few times," says Frenette. "Maranda wouldn't let up on him, and he was depressed when Landry launched his civil action against him. Following several days of cross-examination, where he had to stand for hours on end, I noticed he was suffering from back pain that must have been quite serious. This discouraged him as well. I cheered him up so he'd continue to testify. Other times, the performance of the shares he'd bought would depress him, but I didn't want him to talk to me about that."

The media was following the trial as though it were a soap opera starring Maranda and Quesnel. After several days of cross-examinations, Quesnel glimpsed the light at the end of the tunnel when the lawyer finally questioned him about the plot hatched against Robert Dubuc, for which Vallée had been charged.

"Maranda still had a few surprises in store. One afternoon, just before the trial resumed, the cops in the courthouse hallway noticed five people who resembled me. Those men were wearing the same kind of suit and had the same haircut as me. When the courtroom door was opened, my doubles walked in and blended into the crowd. Judge Jerry Zigman hadn't yet gone up to the bench, and I was sitting in the witness box.

Maranda was looking around the room, and when his gaze fell on me he started laughing. When the jurors and judge arrived, some of the jurors looked astonished. Maranda asked the judge to have me sit with the audience, arguing that he wanted to test the memory of a new witness, a mechanic who'd towed my car a few months earlier. The judge agreed and I went to sit in the audience. It felt rather peculiar. A few bikers were seated around me, but they couldn't do anything, since I had a plainclothes policeman on either side. Then the witness walked in. Maranda started grilling the man, who was very nervous, sweating profusely and shaking. His shirt was drenched. After barely a few minutes, Maranda asked him to turn around and identify me. The witness was obviously confused. The judge asked him to walk up to the person whose vehicle he'd towed. At first, the witness walked up to one of my doubles, then asked the judge if he could look at the man's arm to see if he had tattoos. As my double was about to roll up his sleeves, the judge told him he didn't have to. When the mechanic came up to me, I rolled up my sleeves to show him my arms and he immediately cried out, 'That's him, I'm sure of it!' Maranda then asked the witness if he'd mentioned my tattoos during his meeting with detectives, and he said he had. That's when the lawyer took out the heavy artillery, arguing it was all a plot. He claimed that this part of the evidence had not been provided to him and that this was against the rules. The court agreed with him. Judge Zigman told the jury to disregard the last testimony and to destroy the notes taken during Maranda's performance. The cops hadn't done their jobs properly."

At this point, Quesnel had been testifying for more than twenty days. Exasperated, he asked the judge to intervene to stop the cross-examination.

"Judge Zigman also felt that things were taking forever. He'd ask Maranda if he was nearly done, and the latter would answer, 'Yes, maybe by about 4 P.M.' While testifying, I was constantly looking at the clock. I was very anxious to be done, and my back was sore from standing all the time. When the clock showed 4 P.M., Maranda would open his briefcase and take out a pile of papers filled with questions. He pulled this stunt on me several times. The trial upset me so much that at night I'd answer questions in my dreams. Maranda used all the tricks. One day, he asked me to look around the room at the precise moment Robert Dubuc walked in and saluted Rick Vallée."

" 'Is that the man Mr. Vallée asked you to kill?' the lawyer asked.

" 'Yes,' I answered reluctantly.

"The criminal lawyer had once again scored a point."

At long last, Léo-René Maranda said he was done with the witness. Quesnel breathed a huge sigh of relief, and felt a great weight suddenly lift off his shoulders. Maranda had no witnesses to call for the defence, and the trial was over. Following the judge's statement to the jury, the seven men and four women of the jury withdrew. On Tuesday, December 17, after deliberating for four days, the jury announced that they'd reached a verdict. They had found Rick Vallée not guilty of conspiring to commit murder. In the room, ten or so supporters, mostly members of the Jokers, broke into applause. But Judge Zigman dampened their enthusiasm. Vallée's joy was short-lived. Immediately after the verdict of not guilty was rendered, the biker was taken to another courtroom, where Judge Claire Barrette-Joncas informed him that he was the subject of an extradition request from the American authorities for the murder of Lee Carter, committed on the morning of July 28, 1993, in the small border town of Champlain, New York.

"With everything I saw during that trial, I wasn't surprised by a verdict of not guilty. Maranda had manoeuvred very skilfully to make it my word against Vallée's. The cops made a few mistakes and the jury had no option but to acquit Vallée."

Robert Dubuc, the man who was the target of this alleged plot, was murdered a little more than a year after the end of the trial, at the age of thirty-seven. His bullet-riddled body was found inside a warehouse in Delson. A thirty-two-year-old man who was with him was also killed. The killer or killers remain at large.

After the trial, Quesnel wasn't allowed much time to recharge his batteries. Three weeks later, on January 13, 1997, he was brought back to the witness box to testify against Louis "Melou" Roy and Sudiste. This time, the trial took place in Quebec City. The Crown attorney was Alain Guimond, and the bikers were represented by Jacques Larochelle and Pierre Poupart. Judge Louis de Blois heard the case, which officials had been preparing since the end of November when five hundred prospective jurors were summoned to the courthouse, the most ever summoned. Several of the jury candidates outdid each other in their ingenious reasons for being excused from jury duty. After interviewing 116 people for two full days, officials finally selected a jury comprising seven women and five men. It was a difficult exercise and, even after they had been chosen, some jurors tried to shirk their duty. One woman burst into tears as she was about to sit in the jury box. Another woman started to cry as she reached the bar. The Hells Angels name was having an impact.

"The trial was widely covered by the media and a lot of incredible things were being said. André Arthur, the controversial radio host, enjoyed trying to discredit me. I felt a little less pressure than during the Vallée trial, since I'd acquired some experience with cross-examinations. Maranda had trained me."

Quesnel's father wanted nothing to do with the biker trials. Despite the extensive media reporting, he carefully avoided all reports concerning his son.

"I didn't read a thing, except for an article or two. There was no way I was going to follow those trials. Why? Because it would've hurt and saddened me. I wanted nothing to do with my son's involvement with the bikers. Why should I suddenly take an interest in what he'd experienced while he was with those people?"

Even if the people he dealt with daily knew he was the famous informant's father, no one mentioned a word to him throughout court proceedings.

"The people around me must certainly have talked about it among themselves, but I didn't hear a thing. There were never any questions, insinuations, or criticisms. People respected my silence over my son's actions. I wasn't following the proceedings and didn't want to hear about them. When my son chose crime, I also chose my own direction. I decided to look after myself. Though I wasn't insensitive to what he was doing, I didn't try to find out the details of the life he was leading. There was nothing dignified about it."

On December 14, in the midst of the trial and a month before Serge Quesnel was called to the witness box, a troubling incident occurred. André Bédard, a thirty-one-year-old man likely to testify during the trial, was found dead in his Saint-Romuald home. The most credible theory is that he committed suicide by overdosing. Bédard was the man whom Quesnel left for dead following Jacques Ferland's murder in Grondines. Quesnel had shot him in the chest and head.

Finally, in early January, the trial got underway. "When I walked in the room, I could feel that Melou and Sudiste were looking at me. Our eyes met and I saw theirs were filled with disgust. I tried to avoid looking at them. I began my testimony by again saying how the Hells Angels had recruited me, how much they paid me, and how the Trois-Rivières clubhouse functioned. The defence began cross-examining me on my fourth day in the witness box. Larochelle was especially interested in my stock-market investments and asked me about them. With each detail I revealed, I could see, in the corner of my eye, journalists writing in their notepads."

The trial progressed quickly. Larochelle, unlike Maranda, maintained a good pace throughout his cross-examination. His questions to the star witness were very precise and direct. But on the eighth day of his testimony, Quesnel briefly answered a routine question and inadvertently dropped a bombshell.

"Larochelle asked me whether Richard Jobin had boasted about killing France Alain, and I said he had. But

I didn't take the time to explain myself properly, which got a lot of people worked up. Jobin had indeed told me that he'd killed a woman in the early 1980s. However – and this is what I'd wanted to say – I thought that Jobin had only said this to brag, but that's not how it came across."

The murder of that young woman was a major discussion topic in Quebec City, even in 1997. A journalist and former boyfriend of the woman, Benoit Proulx, was sentenced for the crime before being acquitted by the Court of Appeal in the early 1990s. The saga of France Alain and Benoit Proulx lasted several years, as the former journalist went to the Supreme Court and was awarded more than $2,000,000 in compensation for having been wrongly convicted. This verdict was rendered in 2001. So it's easy to understand why Quesnel's claim caused a media uproar the likes of which are rarely seen in Quebec City.

"Larochelle continued with his questions in the days that followed, and they were getting more and more precise. Once in a while, I'd omit a detail and Larochelle would focus on that point. By being questioned, however, things came back to me. So I added precise details about events. Sometimes I was even pleased with the lawyer's questions. I found him very skilful, and he juggled words very effectively. One day, to influence the jury, he said to me, 'At Donnacona, Coriace believed you, and he nearly died. Delcourt believed you, and he died. Jobin believed you, and he died . . .' and he continued in that vein. His goal was clear. It was as though he were telling the jury, 'You see, if you believe him, you'll die.' I thought he was very proficient."

In mid-February, Quesnel's testimony drew to a close. On his last day in the witness box, barraged with questions on his remuneration as an informant, Quesnel pointed to the two defendants and said, "I didn't steal that money, and I don't care whether they're acquitted or sentenced!"

It was now Pit Caron's turn in the witness box. Two weeks later, the defence surprised everyone by saying they had no further questions for Caron and no other witnesses to call. The trial had been going on for nearly four months. Sixty-five witnesses had been heard, and 165 items or documents had been submitted, including the contracts between the two informants and the Department of Justice. Everything in the defence's summation speeches revolved around the credibility of the informants. The payments made to Serge Quesnel and Michel Caron were also brought up. One of the lawyers defending the bikers, Pierre Poupart, said, "The state is paying crooks."

Once the defence speeches were over, Judge Louis de Blois gave the jury his directives before sending it off to deliberate. The waiting began. On the second day of deliberations, the jurors told the judge that they'd like to review Serge Quesnel's testimony, testimony that lasted fourteen days. Everything indicated that the jurors were far from an agreement. The next day, the jury returned to the courtroom and asked the judge to provide the definition of "reasonable doubt" again. On the fifth day, the jury had a third request, this time for the stenographed notes of Caron's testimony. The suspense continued. Then, on the seventh day, April 9, the jury announced that it had reached a verdict. The rumour that the jury was about to render its decision concerning the biker trial moved through the Quebec City courthouse with lightning speed. A hundred or so people dashed toward the courtroom. Defendants Roy and Sudiste walked in with a determined step, displaying confidence, smiling to the left and right, standing very straight. Then the judge entered. Finally, the seven women and five men jurors solemnly returned to their seats.

In a loud voice, the jury foreman announced that the two Hells Angels were not guilty of the murders of Jacques Ferland and Richard Delcourt. The two bikers had trouble containing their joy, thanking the jurors by nodding in their direction. Even before the jury had left the room, the two bikers hugged and congratulated each other. They saluted the Crown attorney and the detectives surrounding them with broad smiles as they left the courtroom. However, they weren't out of the woods yet. Roy soon learned that he was now charged with murdering Claude "le Pic" Rivard in Montreal, while Sudiste faced new charges of conspiring to commit murder. In the days that followed, the media pointed fingers at the informants, especially at Serge Quesnel, to explain the bikers' acquittal. Journalists wondered why the government was dealing with a man whose credibility was more than questionable.

Quesnel says, "The verdict really didn't surprise me, and I didn't much care about the attacks against me. However, I'd have liked the opportunity to respond to some of the comments made by several journalists and talk-show hosts. The detectives made mistakes, the Crown attorneys as well. And I answered all questions."

As soon as his testimony ended, Quesnel was transferred to the Saint-Jérôme detention centre, a facility that can hold 350 inmates. It was the first time in several months that Quesnel was denied the cozy comforts of QPF cells. Quesnel hadn't expected to return to a detention centre so quickly. He was staggered and needed a few days to get over it. He thought he had been abandoned and deserted. He felt that the wonderful promises made to him hadn't been kept, and remembered the words of reporter Claude Poirier: "After being well pressed, the lemon is thrown away." The authorities had placed him in the section reserved for informants, where they should be safe. One day, however, while he was in an office, talking on the phone, Quesnel got the surprise of his life when he saw a mafia boss walk in. Raymond Fernandez, forty-one years old, was also a prisoner at Saint-Jérôme. Fernandez closed the door and sat down in front of Quesnel.

Born in Spain, Fernandez came to Canada at the age of five. He became driver to the head of the Montreal Mafia, Frank Cotroni, while still very young and was implicated in several crimes. Fernandez made a name for himself on his twenty-first birthday by murdering a seventeen-year-old stripper, by punching, knifing, and hitting her with the legs of a chair. He was convicted and sent to jail, but released after a few years. He was regularly seen in the company of godfather Vito Rizzuto. Then, in 1991, Fernandez was again sentenced, this time for trafficking cocaine. He made the best of a bad situation by getting married in the chapel of the Saint-Anne-des-Plaines penitentiary.

Fernandez lived in jail in grand style. For instance, in the summer of 1994, at Donnacona penitentiary, he paid for a stripper show organized by the inmates. At the time he met Quesnel at the Saint-Jérôme prison, Raymond Fernandez was awaiting trial for importing 450 kilos of hashish. The man who sat in front of Quesnel was no altar boy.

"A detention-centre employee brought him to the room I was in. When I saw him walk in, I was sure he'd attack me. He was an old friend, but the situation had changed with my becoming an informant. I was wondering whether he had a spike, whether he was going to kill me. I was freaking out. My status absolutely precluded me from being in the presence of other prisoners, except for informants. Moreover, a detention-centre employee had put him in direct contact with me. It turned out that Fernandez wanted to corrupt an informant who was living in my wing and offered me $50,000 to talk to this man, who was scheduled to testify against someone linked to the Mafia. All I wanted was for him to leave the room. I acted as though I was confident, but I was in a state of shock. I told Fernandez that I'd talk to the informant in question and he left. As soon as he walked out, I called the QPF. This encounter made a lot of noise internally. The employee who'd set up the meeting was read the riot act by his bosses, and then he had the gall to ask me why I'd alerted the police. Fernandez himself was told what I'd done and called me all sorts of names, through a window. The whole business was very suspicious. I think Fernandez had bribed the employee to get to talk to me."

Raymond Fernandez was deported from Canada in 1999 as a result of his criminal activities and his long police record. In March 2001, however, he was arrested once again when he was spotted in Toronto using the alias of Joe Bravo. He didn't put up any resistance when a SWAT team surrounded him. He was obviously trying to get back into harness with the Mafia.

Although he was now in jail, Quesnel still hadn't finished testifying. Two weeks following the trial of Louis Roy and Sudiste, Mario Lussier's trial began. Lussier was the president of the Rowdy Crew and Quesnel's accomplice in the murder of Claude Rivard in Montreal. Quesnel learned that he would have to face the lawyer Léo-René Maranda once again, and was somewhat worried. Melou Roy, for his part, had been released pending his trial for Rivard's murder. However, he had to post $100,000 in bail and his father had to guarantee a sum of $250,000 to ensure he would appear in court. Roy was forbidden from owning a cellphone or a pager, and was not allowed to travel farther than 150 kilometres from the Saguenay, the region where he was born. Roy was obliged to stay at the Royal Motel, the establishment his father runs in Jonquière. The Crown attorney had filed a list of all bikers affiliated to the Hells Angels with the court, and Roy was prohibited from talking, even by phone, to any of the 180 people on the list.

"When the cops who were taking care of me learned that Judge Jean-Guy Boilard would hear the Lussier case, one of them cried out, 'Not that maniac!' But Inspector Pierre Frenette told me that everything would go

smoothly if I told the truth and was polite. He was right.
In the courtroom, Judge Boilard always kept the situation under control. He was the boss, and Maranda
couldn't do as he pleased. It seemed to me that the judge
took pleasure in putting Maranda in his place. I quickly
found out I wouldn't remain in the witness box forever,
as I had during Vallée's trial. Maranda wasn't as sure of
himself this time. Once, he tried to argue a point of law,
Judge Boilard explained the point in question and told
him in front of everyone: 'Don't try it. You know very
well the law doesn't say that.' It was my turn to look at
the lawyer with a cheeky little smile. When Maranda
elaborated too much on a question, trying to confuse
me while I was giving an explanation, the judge again
intervened, saying, 'That's enough, Mr. Maranda, you've
considered all possible angles of that question, so change
the subject!' At one point Maranda wanted the proceedings suspended because I'd just revealed that
Lussier, the defendant, had told me about another
murder he'd participated in. Maranda was really furious.
Once again, however, Judge Boilard put him in his
place, saying, 'You know what happens when you dig too
much.' I felt that the lawyer was completely destabilized.
No doubt a little frustrated, Maranda uttered an inaudi-
ble comment, but Judge Boilard immediately replied, 'If
you have something to say, Mr. Maranda, get up from

your chair!' To me, it was sweet revenge to see the lawyer who'd manhandled me during the Vallée trial being so resoundingly put in his place."

Once Quesnel had finished testifying, Maranda called other people to the witness box. Crown attorney François Legault confirmed Quesnel's account by filing with the court several Bell Mobility and Cantel bills that proved that Lussier was in almost constant contact with other members of the Angels. The jury of six men and six women deliberated for only sixty minutes before reaching a verdict. Lussier was found guilty of murder. He was given a life sentence, making him eligible for parole only after serving twenty-five years in jail.

Two days after Lussier's trial, Rick Vallée made headlines by staging a spectacular escape. Escorted by two police officers while being treated at Montreal's Saint-Luc Hospital, he managed to overpower his two guards with the help of two armed accomplices and to escape on a motorcycle. He was about to be extradited to the United States to be tried for the murder of Lee Carter. Until he was recaptured on April 18, 2003, in Montreal, Vallée was among the most-wanted criminals in the world. He had returned to Montreal from hiding in Costa Rica (after undergoing plastic surgery) because he was homesick.

After the Lussier trial, Quesnel took advantage of a calm spell. He regularly visited a specialist who was

Police raid the Hells Angels' clubhouse in Trois-Rivières following the informant's confession. (Courtesy of *Allô Police*)

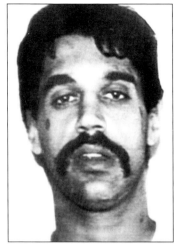

Serge Quesnel later had the distinctive tattoo tears on his face removed. (Courtesy of *Allô Police*)

Quesnel photographed by the police a few weeks before his arrest.

Police officers accompany Quesnel on his way to court. (Courtesy of *Allô Police*)

This provocative photograph of Sandra Beaulieu when she visited Quesnel at QPF headquarters in Quebec City was published in *Le Soleil* newspaper. It touched off a storm of controversy over the conditions in which the killer was being held. (Courtesy of *Allô Police*)

Beaulieu and Quesnel.

This photograph of Louis "Melou" Roy, president of the Trois-Rivières chapter of the Hells Angels, was taken in the mid-1990s. Melou disappeared on June 24, 2000. (Courtesy of *Allô Police*)

Richard "Rick" Vallée, a full-patch member of the Hells Angels, escaped from police custody on June 5, 1997, and disappeared for several years. He eventually returned to Montreal, feeling homesick, and was recaptured on April 18, 2003.

The .357 magnum revolver used to kill Richard Delcourt. Delcourt's body was found at the edge of Highway 363 between Saint-Casimir and Saint-Ubalde in the county of Portneuf.

Richard Delcourt's house in Sainte-Thècle, in the Mauricie.

The house where Jacques Ferland was killed in Grodines, located between Trois-Rivières and Quebec City.

gradually removing his tattoos by using a laser. Since Quesnel had tattoos all over his arms, the total cost of the operation would be more than $20,000. The rest of the time, still imprisoned at Saint-Jérôme, Quesnel worried about his fate. Not because he was testifying against the bikers, but because he felt unsafe in detention. The authorities weren't honouring certain clauses of his contract and he could run into another inmate at any time. He felt he was facing numerous risks of being attacked.

"I decided to sue the government. I contacted a Quebec City lawyer, Guy Bertrand, to explain the facts. He understood that I wasn't imprisoned in an area suited to my situation, as stipulated in my contract. I didn't try to conceal that I had hired a lawyer, and it soon came to the attention of the centre's management. One day, the employee who was behind my misadventure with Fernandez started tongue-lashing me in front of everybody for complaining without reason. While preparing my lawsuit, I applied for a transfer to another detention centre. I didn't want to stay at Saint-Jérôme."

During this time, Quesnel was still on good terms with many of the policemen who were handling his file. He even considered some of them to be friends, although he saw that many of them were only playing the role of "good guys," and were scorning him as soon as his back was turned.

"One day, I called the QPF in Montreal to get information on a murder. It was a collect call. While the automated system was delivering its message to the policeman who'd picked up the receiver, I heard him say, 'Oh no! Not that son of a bitch again!' He accepted the charges. Once the link was established, the same cop blurted out: 'Hi! How's it going? Been a long time since we heard from you!' Seething with anger, I didn't say a word and hung up. Those words opened my eyes. I realized I was considered a lowlife, only a flunky helping them to make arrests. Fortunately, other cops were honest with me from beginning to end. Some ask for news of me to this day."

Two weeks after the end of Lussier's trial, in June 1997, Serge Quesnel was taken to the Shawinigan courthouse. He was scheduled to testify in the trial of Sudiste, now charged with conspiracy to murder René Guillet, a resident of La Tuque. These trips between Saint-Jérôme and Shawinigan continued until mid-July, when Judge Jacques Trudel declared, in his turn, that Sudiste's lawyer was ineligible to defend him. This was another victory for Quesnel, who was, once again, facing the lawyer who introduced him to the Hells Angels. When the court set the date for Sudiste's preliminary hearing in the fall, the deposed lawyer announced that Jacques Larochelle would defend the biker instead.

Quesnel didn't really care who the defence lawyer would be. He had other concerns and was getting more and more worried and nervous. In the wing where he was kept at Saint-Jérôme, the atmosphere was turbulent. The restlessness was palpable. The authorities, not knowing how to react, stuffed the informants with sedatives. Still, fights broke out among the inmates.

"It was becoming crazy. All we did was watch TV. We were allowed to go to the gym for one hour a day. The rest of the time, nothing! The atmosphere was heavy, and we continually had the impression our neighbours were in our personal space. We were cooped up like chickens. When moving around, we were increasingly coming into contact with other inmates. For instance, the place where we got haircuts was next to a wing where all inmates hated informants. From the way things were being run, it was obvious that the authorities were improvising. When I called the cops to complain that my contract wasn't being honoured, they referred me to Correctional Services, who referred me to the Public Security Department, and so on. They were all passing the buck."

During this time, Quesnel had to make several trips to Quebec City. His former accomplice, Nose, had been charged with the murders of Richard Jobin and Martin Naud, and the groundwork for his trial was being prepared. And who better than Serge Quesnel to get him convicted?

"The QPF had put new detectives in charge of the case and they didn't much care for subtleties. They wanted to get Nose convicted and didn't care what means were used. Let's just say we didn't get along. I'd forgotten a few details and the two new detectives didn't appreciate this. I wasn't the best collaborator."

On August 4, Quesnel's wish was granted. He was transferred from Saint-Jérôme to Valleyfield, a place he called an informants' paradise.

"There were six or seven of us informants in the same wing and we enjoyed several privileges. We had private showers, a washbasin, and two fridges that were always stocked with food. We also had our own stove. The authorities provided the food, since the other inmates usually cooked all the meals and informants risked being poisoned. We designated two guys to do the cooking. We managed very well, making meals and then drinking, as we were able to get our hands on homemade alcohol even there. But incidents occurred once in a while."

The informants in that wing, most of them men who had killed for the bikers, made headlines in April 1998, when prison guards had to intervene to calm three of them down for partying too loudly. Their names: Serge Quesnel, Stéphane Alain, and Ronnie Marcogliese. The three men were high and the music was deafening.

Marcogliese was so bold as to tap one of the jailers on the stomach. The Valleyfield guards took advantage of this incident to denounce their difficult working conditions.

Quesnel says, "We certainly were comfortable there. A section of the yard was set aside just for us. I spent a couple of thousand dollars on barbells so that the guys could train. At one point, I was even set to bring in tanning beds, but the deal fell through. Even with all this happening, I still managed to pass two correspondence courses, although I sometimes had trouble concentrating because the guys liked to party. I took those courses to relieve the boredom, since I had nothing else to do."

Quesnel had been in Valleyfield for three weeks when he found out, at the same time as everyone else, that his former boss, Melou Roy, had been the victim of an attempted murder. Roy was returning to his father's motel in Jonquière when he was riddled with bullets as he was getting out of his car. He was hit in the lungs, liver, and legs, but managed to pull through after a few hours on the operating table. The police guarded the room of the famous biker for a few days. But when members of the Nomads refused to cooperate in the investigation, the authorities decided to stop protecting Roy.

"Melou may have been shot because of me. He hired me and was responsible for my actions. When I crossed over to the police camp, I dragged the organization through the mud. Perhaps they had decided to eliminate him, or maybe some other people had a grudge against him. Melou likely rankled a lot of people during his career."

In Valleyfield, life went on. Quesnel and his friends had a lot of leeway and could do pretty much as they pleased inside their wing. At the time, his stock market investments were earning him thousands of dollars. So he decided to live it up.

"I bought a home theatre and a large leather chair. It was the lap of luxury. My cellmates were envious, so I agreed to lend money to several of them. Those I lent $6,000 to, would pay me back $7,000. Everyone had a home theatre. It was incredible. Naturally, this didn't suit the guards and caused friction, but I honestly didn't care. I was taking advantage of my money and that's all. However, one of the informants never repaid me the $1,000 I'd lent him. I even tried to take him to small claims court, but he wasn't solvent. I decided to give up. The guy had such poor credibility that officials even withdrew the benefits he enjoyed as an informant."

Despite the luxury, the atmosphere on the wing was tempestuous. Informants were always on the alert. Anxiety constantly ate away at these men who were confined to rather cramped spaces. Then something happened that did little to reassure Quesnel and his buddies.

"One night, a guard named Karine opened the small panel on the door of our section. We immediately noticed that Karine wasn't in her normal state. She was very nervous and kept looking behind her. She then blurted out: 'Quick, call the police. A man is shooting a submachine gun in the jail.' Without saying another word, she ran off. We panicked. I asked myself, Why don't they call the cops themselves? Are they all dead? The way this prison was built, it would be easy to steal the keys to different sections and take control of the entire building. I immediately thought the attack was directed at us, the informants. For the first time in my life, I seriously thought I was going to die. I was a Hells Angels star informant, and there were numerous reasons to kill me. I wasted no time. I smashed a wooden chair, grabbed one of its legs, and hid beside the door that gave access to our wing. I was with another informant. We wanted to try to knock out the armed man. But the latter was trapped when the guards managed to surround him. They'd activated the automatic door locks from the control station. The man, named Blanchette, had escaped while one of the guards was temporarily absent; he was linked to the Rockers, a Hells Angels puppet club. When the guards managed to bring him under control, they noticed he was drunk. This was fortunate, since I think he could have easily hit us had he been sober."

The atmosphere remained hot at the Valleyfield prison during the autumn, and the informants passed

the time as best they could. Quesnel spent his days studying, partying, and carefully watching the fluctuations of
his stock market investments. In September, he testified
against Nose, his former partner, about the murders of
Richard Jobin and Martin Naud.

"The first time I was brought into the courtroom
to testify, Nose was in his own world, in a delirium,
laughing for no reason. As I was testifying, his attitude
gradually changed. His expression hardened, and I could
feel his anger. It was peculiar. His two sisters were in the
audience, and I could see the hatred in their eyes.
I'd been a kind of hero to Nose's sisters, but it was a
completely different story now. To them, I'd become
a slimebag, a bastard. My ex-girlfriend, Chantal, didn't
attend the proceedings. I don't know how I would have
reacted with her in the courtroom."

Then, on September 25, 1998, there was a dramatic
turn of events, when Judge Jean-Claude Beaulieu
ordered that proceedings against Nose be stayed. His
lawyer, Christiane Filteau, asked for this stay after
learning that the Sainte-Foy police had destroyed evidence. Judge Beaulieu had found out that a detective
with the Sainte-Foy police had destroyed a knife, a pair
of scissors, and a shoelace used to strangle Martin
Naud. A beginner's blunder. Consternation swept
through the courtroom. Nose's girlfriend and his sisters
shed tears of joy.

"Nose was set free, and I was furious at the Sainte-Foy police for being such amateurs. I even made a statement to the media. My former lawyer had been right when he suggested I should commit crimes in Sainte-Foy because there would be far fewer risks of being caught."

The municipal police aren't the only ones to be blamed over this business. In his decision, Judge Beaulieu highlighted that the QPF had omitted to follow through properly with the Sainte-Foy police.

The dust was just beginning to settle after Nose's trial when something very surprising happened. Five of the bikers against whom Serge Quesnel was scheduled to testify pleaded guilty, and three of them surrendered to the QPF in Quebec City. They were Mario Brouillette, twenty-five years old; François Hinse, thirty-three; and Clermont Carrier, thirty-five, a member of the Mauricie Blatnois. The two others – Sylvain Thiffault, forty, and Claude Giguère, thirty-six – were already in jail.

Brouillette had been on the run since December 6, 1995, and pleaded guilty to being an accessory after the fact in the murder of Claude Rivard. He had driven Quesnel to the murder scene and had disposed of certain evidence, earning a six-year sentence for his trouble. Hinse admitted to conspiring to kill Rock Machine member Gino Hallé in the Quebec City region in November 1994. He'd been wanted since December 1994, and got four years. Giguère pleaded guilty to participating in the same conspiracy with Hinse, getting two years less a day, since he was already remanded in custody. Thiffault admitted to conspiring to murder René Guillet, the La Tuque hotel-keeper who was, apparently, a drug dealer for the Rock Machine. (Guillet had been sentenced to eight months in jail for setting fire to his cottage. When he set the fire, Guillet did not know that his sixteen-year-old son was inside the cottage. The youth died in the blaze.) Thiffault was sentenced to six years in jail, but had to serve only two years less a day, because of the time he'd spent remanded in custody. Finally, Carrier pleaded guilty to the charge of conspiring to murder another hotel-keeper, Stéphane Bernard, and received a four-year sentence.

The news delighted Quesnel. At last, his credibility had been somewhat re-established. But his joy vanished when he learned the motives behind these confessions. An agreement had been reached between the bikers and the Crown, and, in exchange for all these confessions, the murder charge against Melou Roy was dropped. The deal was negotiated between Jacques Larochelle, the brilliant lawyer who already saved Roy's skin during a sensational trial in Quebec City, and lawyers from the Department of Justice. Roy wouldn't have to stand trial for the murder of Claude Rivard.

"I was very upset and disgusted when I learned that Melou got off in exchange for confessions from the other bikers, especially because I heard about it from the media and not from the police. I thought it was unusual and resented the cops for this, as well as the Crown attorneys who'd made the deal. They were letting the most important player get away. Once again Melou had managed to get off scot-free. My only consolation was that the confessions of the other bikers proved my claims. They confirmed that I had some credibility as an informant."

"The deal wasn't bad at all," says Insp. Pierre Frenette. "We really weren't sure Melou would be found guilty in the upcoming trial. Nothing could be taken for granted. As well, we would have had to try the five guys who surrendered, with all the efforts and costs involved. We couldn't take anything for granted in their cases, either. They would have involved several more testimonies from Serge Quesnel. So, given all these factors, the deal was acceptable. Anyhow, Melou probably got his sentence, as it were."

Like many people, Frenette thinks that Melou Roy is dead. No one has seen him since June 24, 2000. According to the most plausible theory, he was murdered by one of his "brothers." The rented Mercedes that Roy had been driving was found in downtown Montreal three weeks after his disappearance. As well, police learned that the contents of his bank account, some $500,000, had been shared among his "brothers." If Roy was murdered, as is likely, it remains to be determined whether Quesnel's betrayal of the bikers had anything to do with it, since Roy was morally responsible for him in the eyes of the Hells Angels. Roy may also have been killed because others were jealous that he made a great deal of money. Another possibility is that some bikers may not have liked going to jail in his place. Did he die as a result of one or some of these reasons? His close relatives, including his wife, the mother of his two children, have never filed a complaint over his disappearance.

Now Quesnel would not have to testify against Roy. However, he was called to testify against the leader of the Nomads, Maurice "Mom" Boucher, in the fall of 1998 after Boucher was charged with ordering the murder of two prison guards. This was Boucher's first trial.

"My testimony was very brief, some twenty minutes at most. I was asked to tell the story of the five months I'd spent with the Hells Angels to the six men and six women of the jury. Jacques Larochelle also cross-examined me, but things went smoothly. At first, I didn't want to testify against Boucher. I had nothing to say about him, because I'd hardly ever associated with him. However, I was forced to testify. My testimony was intended to help enhance the value of another inform-ant in the case. It was brief, but I had enough time to spot several bikers in the audience. Boucher himself was looking at me sideways. I was glad when it was over. I was fed up with courts, testimonies, lawyers' questions, onlookers, detectives. I'd done my part. At that point, I only wanted to serve my sentence and move on to some-thing else. I wanted to make a fresh start and leave the world of bikers forever. It was time to start building my future. Obviously, you can't erase everything at once. Psychologically, I had work to do. I first had to rebuild my self-esteem and find the tools needed to overhaul my life completely. At that point, at the end of 1998, I still had a lot of time ahead of me, as I had nearly ten years yet to serve. That gives you a lot of time to think!"

5

REDEMPTION

I FIRST MET SERGE QUESNEL shortly before Christmas 2001 and was initially at a complete loss about how to behave. He'd called me in November 2001, asking whether I wanted to tell the story of his life, and I'd agreed. Though we'd often spoken on the phone, it had taken me two months to get permission from the Public Security Department to meet him. Since December, I'd seen him nearly every Sunday and, in theory, my last meeting with him was to take place on March 10, 2002.

Quesnel was an important player at the beginning of the present biker war. The Hells Angels had used him as though he were a toy, but that toy blew up in their face. The former killer has now served half his sentence, and is getting ready to die, as it were. When he is released in 2007, he'll no longer be Serge Quesnel. He'll have a new identity, a new face, a new body. His numerous tattoos, the vestiges of his earlier and more turbulent life, will all have been removed. This book is, in a way, his last will and testament as Serge Quesnel. He's decided to tell all, to completely purge himself of the underworld, a world he'll never see again.

On that day in March, I was sitting in the small room set aside for us. I barely had enough time to pull out the tape recorder and plug it in before Quesnel arrived. As usual, he shook my hand. I wasn't worried. Over the previous weeks, I had got to know Quesnel, and considered him to be intelligent, quick-witted, but also anxious. He would turn around every time a door opened. The gesture was never nervous, only mechanical. It was the reaction of a man who's condemned to take no risks. Ever. Then he'd continue talking. Quesnel loved to talk, and it seemed to be good for him.

At our March meeting, he poured his heart out, telling me what life was like for him. Completely isolated from other inmates, he is sometimes discouraged. The other informants no longer live in the same wing, so he is alone and cut off from everything. Any other prisoner would be sent to the hole for a few weeks after breaking a rule, but Quesnel is isolated like that all the time. Prison officials say that this is to ensure his safety. However, a special clause was included in his contract, stipulating that he wouldn't be forgotten deep in some prison wing. At the time, he was even told that setting up a special wing for informants was being considered, but it never happened.

The only thing Serge Quesnel does is study. He's taking university courses by correspondence and has a gift for studying. His marks confirm this, as he gets mostly A's. Not bad for someone who hadn't even completed high school. Quesnel knows that studying is his only way out and has decided to devote himself to it completely.

"I want to get a Ph.D. When I'm released in 2007, I'll have money to start a business, but if things don't go well, I'll have the tools needed to pull through. I'll be able to start a new life outside of crime. I never again want to feel the pressure I went through. I can never return to crime, because I'm a dead man if I do. So I'm taking all the steps needed to secure my future. I'll even go and live outside Quebec. I'm bilingual. I'll make a fresh start. I probably won't ever see my parents again, since I don't really have a choice. When I'll meet a woman, she won't know where I'm from. The same goes for the people around me. I'll never say a thing. It's a question of survival."

◎

December 20, 2001. I had just had dinner with a publisher who was interested in the story of Serge Quesnel.

He had even offered us a contract. Following this meeting, I headed over to meet Quesnel for the first time. On the way, I wondered how things would go. I'd already spoken to him, since he had called me several times. But writing the story of his life was a considerable challenge. I wanted to tell him from the outset exactly what I intended to do: "Listen, I'll write the story of your criminal life, but there's no way I'm going to polish your image. If that's what you expect, then you've knocked at the wrong door." Quesnel seemed surprised by the warning. He reassured me and said he wanted the full story to be written. He looked at the contract offered by the publisher. Although I felt its terms were generous, Quesnel wasn't completely satisfied. He was sure he could get a better deal. I was surprised. This was my first foray into book publishing, and I couldn't imagine demanding better terms. But Quesnel insisted. He was afraid of being swindled. Somewhat reluctantly, I told him I'd go back to the publisher and see what I could do. Eventually, he managed to get the publisher to improve the terms of the offer. He's a skilful negotiator, as the government and the publisher found out. He knows what he wants, and he wants a lot. He's demanding of himself and of others.

Our first meeting went smoothly. I asked him a few questions to see how far he'd go in revealing his secrets and quickly found out that Quesnel was sincere when he said he wanted to hide nothing. I recorded everything, and he had no objections. This augured well.

Starting in January 2002, Serge Quesnel told me the story of his life. We talked about the bikers, prison, murders, police, fights, and criminals, as well as about women. He seemed very confident about his future and was looking forward to it. Since he turned eighteen, he has spent less than two years out of prison, but he's convinced he'll make a success of his new life. And he has lots of time to think about it. Thinking is the only thing you can do in jail, and sometimes you go crazy while doing so. Quesnel passes the time as best he can.

"Once all the trials were over, everyone forgot about me. I no longer had any contact with the cops or the attorneys, and was now the responsibility of the Public Security Department. I soon realized that all the things I'd been promised were only empty words. The government had told me I'd be living in a place adapted to my situation. But this wasn't so, and they didn't know what to do with me. I was isolated in every sense of the word. Things really smacked of improvisation. I realized life wouldn't be easy. Right from the outset, at the Saint-Jérôme prison, I was placed in a situation where I came across other inmates. It happened again on several occasions following the Fernandez incident. I felt my life was in danger. So I asked lawyer Guy Bertrand to file a suit against the authorities. Contrary to what I'd been promised, nothing was adapted to my situation. In Valleyfield, things had gone well at first, but soured afterwards. But now I was in litigation with the government, and was transferred to a federal prison."

Quesnel was taken to the Special Handling Unit at Sainte-Anne-des-Plaines, where he was placed in isolation. Once again, it was as though he were in the hole. He had contact with no one. Things were different there, however, since no one owed or had promised him anything. Surprisingly, it was a fellow inmate who made his life most difficult.

"I went through hell in the two years I spent in that federal prison, which housed the worst criminals in Canada. My neighbour insulted me constantly. He made noise continually for two long years to prevent me from sleeping at night. But the guards were good to me. They understood what that seventy-four-year-old inmate was putting me through. But their situation was even worse than mine. My neighbour regularly threw his excrement at the guards' faces. But prison administrators had no other place to put me, since I was in the most secure section."

At Sainte-Anne-des-Plaines, Quesnel spent his time as best he could, trying to forget his surly neighbour. He also pursued his lawsuit against the government for failing to respect its contract with him. Government officials got to find out that this guy is hard-headed.

"The authorities knew very well I was right. I'd realized I was going away for a long time, so I'd negotiated a clause stipulating that I was to be held in a place adapted to my situation. The other informants didn't have such a clause. All the authorities could offer me were practically abandoned leftover sections or the hole. They finally admitted they were wrong. The Attorney General of Quebec offered me $30,000 as compensation, which I accepted since I was at the end of my tether at Sainte-Anne-des-Plaines. I wanted to get out of there because it had become unbearable. I also agreed because I had to repay a line of credit on my stock market investments. As soon as I accepted the government's offer, I automatically returned to being the responsibility of the province. I was transferred to the Sherbrooke detention centre, on Talbot Street."

In the agreement signed on March 6, 2001, the Quebec government offered Quesnel $30,000 simply to prevent the matter from going to trial. The government also agreed to foot the bill for any additional costs that Quesnel may be ordered to pay as a result of the verdict in Landry's case, which was being appealed. The agreement also stipulated that Quesnel had to be sent back to a provincial detention centre to respect the contract signed in June 1995. At Sherbrooke, Quesnel had new problems to face.

"One of the guards thought she was my mother and continually lectured me. I ended up hating her. One day, while talking to her, I got my own back. She messed up by telling me a simple anecdote.

"'My spouse saw you on TV,' she said.

"'How come your spouse knows you're taking care of me? Did you tell him?' I asked.

"She turned white as a bedsheet, knowing she'd just blundered. No one was supposed to know where I was. A directive had been issued stipulating that detention centre employees were never to reveal my whereabouts. I wrote the director, asking for a transfer, complaining of my guard's 'dangerous' behaviour, specifying that my safety was at stake. The guard was furious when she found out that I'd complained to the director and came over to my wing. She criticized me for involving her family. She was aggressive and completely distraught. I told her that members of her family would be called to testify if I took the matter to court. She didn't think this was funny. In the days that followed, she set the other guards against me and the authorities had no other choice but to transfer me."

Quesnel had burned his bridges in Sherbrooke and was no longer welcome. Nor was he welcome in other centres. He was taken from one place to the other, and the clause specifying his prison conditions in his contract still wasn't being honoured. Once again, he was in a position to sue the government. In the agreement signed in 2001, when Quesnel was given $30,000, the government forgot to stipulate that he couldn't file further lawsuits about the conditions of his detention. His father is convinced the government will never completely respect the 1995 agreement.

"They won't honour his contract. In the time he's been in prison, we've seen there's no room for him anywhere. He can file all the lawsuits he wants against bureaucrats, but he'll never be in the right. He didn't make any friends, and those people have complete control over him. He isn't in a position to negotiate anything and the decision-makers are fully aware of this. When he contacts a lawyer to try to get his claim heard, he's given the runaround. The few privileges he has are taken away and, in the end, he's completely discouraged. Officials ask him to become a good citizen, to behave properly and to be honest, but they don't shy away from breaking the agreement where the conditions of his detention are concerned. I really don't see how he can win this battle against the authorities. It's somewhat like David and Goliath, but David won't win this time."

Insp. Pierre Frenette agrees with Quesnel's father. "There's no room for a guy like Quesnel, and we had lots of problems with the prisons. At first, some of the smaller centres were willing to take him in, to help prevent them from being closed, while others wanted nothing to do with him. In other places, prison officials took him in with some reluctance, as many guards consider informants to be less than worthless. They don't want to have any problems with them, and having good relations with an informant is frowned on. So informants are frequently put in the hole, which is often run by guards who want nothing to do with inmates, guards who are practically unable to do their jobs among the 'normal' prison population."

Quesnel says, "I sometimes go through difficult periods. Isolation weighs me down and studying is all I do. I seriously got back into it in Sherbrooke. Since then I've had excellent marks, rarely below 90 per cent. Teachers often congratulate me, saying I'm one of their best students. I'm now doing a bachelor's degree in administration, spending some forty hours a week at my books. It's better for my mental health than following the stock market."

Quesnel knows what he's talking about. At the beginning of his sentence, he was fixated on the fate of his shares. He'd invested his money in the stock market and was scrupulously following its least fluctuations. He was obsessed.

"When I began to invest, I quickly made money. Some tens of thousands of dollars in a few months. And that's when I got caught. I thought it would always be easy. I wanted to rake in a lot, so I wagered a lot. I wasn't

the type to diversify assets. Then things began tumbling
down. Nortel cost me a bundle, a little more than
$100,000. Though I'd had a great deal of success in the
previous months, I was badly disappointed in this case.
I'd wanted to outwit the system, but it was impossible.
At first, I called a company that put me in touch with a
broker, who didn't have much experience and gave me
bad advice. He should have checked my fervour, but he
didn't. I was hounding him, calling him every day,
continually asking him about market trends. Every
morning, I'd read the paper, look at stock market results,
then phone him. I wanted to know why things were
going down, if they'd rise again, and when. I criticized
him for getting me to invest in such or such a company.
I contested his projections and put a lot of pressure on
him. The poor guy didn't know which way to turn.
Moreover, since my name had often been mentioned in
the press, he knew exactly who I was. Over the weeks,
he grew more and more nervous, but I didn't let up on
him. One day, my broker's boss answered the phone. He
informed me that the broker was on sick leave due to a
burnout, and asked me how much it would cost his
office for me to change brokers. I told him I wanted
$2,000, and he agreed. His employee had made me lose
money due to his inexperience. I changed brokers, to a
woman this time. It would cost me dearly.

"I started making huge transactions, since I had a lot of money. She should have slowed me down, but she didn't. And then the market crashed. It opened my eyes, and I fired my broker. I've now changed my way of doing things. All my investments are guaranteed. That way, I know I won't lose any money. I contact my broker now and again, but am no longer obsessed with doing so. I don't watch the stock market like I did at first. It's better for my health."

"Serge is a guy who likes high risks," says his father. "So it was only natural for him to make risky investments. Once again he didn't ask anyone's advice, wanting to outsmart the system himself. The attraction of money was very strong. However, he accepted the consequences of the risks he took."

Everyone knows that Quesnel has signed a lucrative contract with the government, and it's only normal that some people would try to take advantage of his small fortune. And this is what a complete stranger tried to do.

"I was attending a meeting of Alcoholics Anonymous. A group from outside the prison would come to see us. A young woman with the group came up to me and asked whether I could help her. She needed a few thousand dollars to settle her personal problems. I refused."

Quesnel no longer attends AA meetings and claims he has no problem with alcohol. He used to go just to meet people. It was good for him at the time, but no longer. Today, his only focus is studying.

"I don't even work out physically any more, since I understood that the solution to my problems is to be found inside my head, not in my arms. I used to spend my whole time in prison lifting weights, but I no longer get anything out of it. I prefer to train my mind. It'll be more useful to me."

"Since he left the Sherbrooke prison," says his father, "Serge has jumped back into studying. He devotes all his time to it. I haven't seen his marks, but he tells me they're very good. And so much the better for him."

When I met him on March 10, 2002, the thirty-one-year-old inmate was more withdrawn. His mood was gloomy. The man before me was fed up. He wanted to sue the government again and had contacted a lawyer. He would have preferred to negotiate an out-of-court agreement with the authorities, but that was impossible. He was at daggers drawn with the Public Security Department official who is responsible for him. Quesnel even recorded an excerpt of a conversation he had with a woman from the department who admitted that his prison conditions don't correspond to what's stipulated in the contract. The official knew she was being recorded, but she was furious with Quesnel when he threatened to use part of the recording in his next lawsuit. Communications between them are now completely cut off. Quesnel wanted assurances that he would be given all the tools he needs to reach a high level of education. He was afraid someone would thwart his plans. He was anxious and had even argued with the prison nurse. He wanted to change his medication, which, in his view, was inadequate. She wouldn't hear of it, and voices were raised. The doctor finally sided with Quesnel.

These events may seem trivial to ordinary people, but they contributed to upsetting Quesnel. With me, however, Serge Quesnel was neither threatening nor aggressive. While talking and even expressing his anger, he managed to smile. He then plunged back into talking about the past for the purposes of this book, going back over his criminal life, analyzing his actions and those of others. He is convinced he'd be dead today had he continued his criminal ways and not been arrested. His flamboyant lifestyle would likely have cost him his life. In the world of bikers, those who succeed too quickly are viewed with suspicion. Quesnel is realistic and sees things clearly.

"I've had time to analyze my behaviour since I started serving this sentence. At first, it wasn't very helpful, but it certainly is now. I'm on the way to rehabilitation. I believe that higher education is my only way out. It's the only way I can get away from crime, and I won't let anything stop me. If I find a stimulating work environment when I get out, thanks to the knowledge

I'll have acquired, I'll stand a much better chance of succeeding in my new life. However, if all I find is work as a dishwasher or cook's assistant, I might get discouraged after a few months. I know I have the qualities I need to succeed. Besides, the latest reports from experts are rather flattering to me."

And how! On February 21, 2002, at the request of the Public Security Department, Quesnel agreed to undergo a complete personality assessment. This wasn't the first time he'd been assessed, but he decided to take it seriously this time, which hadn't always been the case.

"In previous assessments, I answered any old how, as I was in a hurry to be done. This time, I decided to answer all questions to the best of my ability, and I think the results surprised many people in the prison world."

The psychologist who handed in her final report on March 4, 2002, drew the following conclusion: "Mr. Quesnel displays an intelligence that is far above average. He is capable of studying at the doctoral level. Thanks to a prison program, he is already doing undergraduate studies and is getting excellent results. Moreover, he has shown a great deal of motivation to study at the graduate level. That would be desirable, since it is very important to invest such potential in positive plans to ensure his self-actualisation and personal fulfilment."

Further on, the report says that Serge Quesnel has "good social identification" and a desire to change for the better. The psychologist also mentions his anxiety, which she attributes to his total isolation.

Naturally, Quesnel is flattered by the results of the assessment, and he's encouraged and determined to continue studying. The purpose of this report was for those who deal with him to better understand Quesnel, as he may soon start being permitted temporary leave, and spend some days outside the detention centre in preparation for his final release.

"That report proves to me that there are no limits to my learning ability, and I'm going to build on that base. It's very encouraging. It shows that I have to busy my mind with positive things. I'm determined to make a fresh start and to live an honest life. Anyhow, I could never again live with the pressure of wondering whether I'll be caught. Nor could I hurt people and live in that rotten world. I'm through with crime."

Since he has been in prison, Serge Quesnel has been subjected to several assessments. A few of them are negative. Either he didn't feel like cooperating with the experts, or else he'd taken a sudden dislike to them. Quesnel can't stand people who look down on him, and when this happens, he can't be counted on to pull his punches. In 1999, while in a federal prison, he was assessed by a French criminologist.

In his thirteen-page report, the specialist described Quesnel as an unusual case, a man who wants to prove himself and to change for the better. The specialist said that he discovered a man completely different from the one who experienced a dazzling rise in the crime world between the ages of nineteen and twenty-four.

"Broken by the confrontation he was subjected to between the underworld and the police who were supporting him during the trial," the criminologist wrote, "Quesnel repented, and even displayed contrition. Far be it for me to have been manipulated by him."

In the same document, the expert summarized other psychological reports concerning Serge Quesnel:

"1992: a psychologist claims he is sound of mind, not delusional, not psychotic, lucid and very well oriented. However, she says he's immature and antisocial.

"1998: a psychotherapist who saw him in August speaks of him as having beneficial synergy.

"1998: in December, a psychologist draws a detailed portrait of Serge Quesnel. To describe his crimes, she speaks of self-actualization, blind obedience, a lack of moral reasoning, escalating violence to get accepted, and of a narcissistic personality. She concludes her report by mentioning his above-average learning potential, and his search for constructive methods for pulling himself out of his depression."

In his 1999 report, the French criminologist wrote: "Quesnel displays the strength seen in some individuals which could allow him to change for the better."

With all these reports before him, Serge Quesnel remains realistic. He doesn't swagger, far from it.

"The important thing isn't what these people have discovered about me, nor what I am on paper, nor what I've done. I'm paying for that now. The important thing is what I'll do in the future. Nothing else matters. I know I can make a positive contribution to society. I'll make amends and I'll be able to do something good. I've done a lot of bad things, hurt a lot of people. I want to make a positive contribution, but don't know if I'm psychologically ready. I'm now seeing a psychologist once a week, and our exchanges are very constructive. The guy is nice, but during our first meetings I didn't open up very much. In fact, I didn't trust him much at first, since he's paid by the government and writes reports for those people. At times, I was afraid I was saying too much and that this might harm my chances of getting temporary leave. But we eventually established mutual confidence. I understood that he was there to help me. In 2000, a specialist determined I was suffering from post-traumatic stress symptoms: difficulty sleeping, anxiety, lack of motivation, flashbacks, problems caused by my isolation and the tension I was subjected to when the authorities allowed other inmates to come into contact with me. This is why I've been prescribed medication."

To pull through, Serge Quesnel is also counting on support from his parents, who have never abandoned him. But, above all, Quesnel relies on himself. He alone is responsible for what happened to him, and he alone can change things.

"I know that the public is entitled to assurances I won't kill again. All I can say is that I feel like a war veteran. I've lost my taste for killing. I'm sorry for the murders I've committed and never again want to do anything that could harm someone. I'll never kill again. I regret the things I've done, but they were done in the context of a gang war. I never killed an honest citizen. Those men I killed knew the rules of the game. I'm not trying to exonerate myself, but only to put things in a better perspective. I'm not the monster certain people have said I am. I still have very precise flashbacks of my crimes. I can still see Martin Naud's corpse at my feet. I often see myself killing my victims. It's like a bad dream, with the action taking place in slow motion. I also realize that I never looked at my victims' faces at the precise moment I killed them. I looked elsewhere, seeking to escape in my own way. All those events are rooted inside me, and I'll live with those images till the day I die."

Quesnel is trying to get rid of everything that links him to his life with the bikers. However, once the trials were over, the QPF detective who'd promised to give him an authentic Hells Angels flag kept his word, bringing him the police's hunting trophy.

"I hung it up in my cell for a few days. It was rather paradoxical for me to end up with this biker emblem. The flag was identical to the ones that fly over club-house roofs. But I finally realized I didn't belong to the Hells Angels, and the flag constantly reminded me that there was a contract on my head. It also reminded me of the harm I'd done. Though it's easy to change a man's civil identity, changing his psychological identity requires more work. After a while, I decided to make a complete break with my previous life. With help from a few guards, I had the Angels flag burned."

Quesnel now only owns one object that reminds him of his previous life with the bikers – a large gold chain, which he wants to sell.

"I bought this piece of jewellery in Quebec City. My pockets were full of money, since Melou had just given me a couple thousand dollars. I walked into a jewellery store and started looking at the showcases. I wanted to buy something flashy and finally noticed a large gold bracelet. I signalled the jeweller to come over and told him I wanted a chain made exactly like the bracelet. He didn't have one, so I asked him to weld two bracelets together to make a chain. The jeweller gave me a funny look. But since I had a lot of money and was paying cash, he didn't need much coaxing. And that's the chain I'm wearing around my neck."

At the beginning of our meeting in March 2002, Quesnel didn't say much. Then I mentioned his early years in prison and he suddenly opened up, talking about the parties he organized. His little fiestas, as he calls them.

"At the beginning of my sentence, I treated myself to a little 'trip' once in a while.

"For a few days, I wouldn't take the pills I was given to fight anxiety. I'd gather them up for two or three days, then swallow the whole lot on Friday. This didn't pose any risks for my health, but it knocked me out, and helped me unwind a little."

"That's often the way it is in jail," says Pierre Frenette. "Besides, I think inmates are given too many pills. Prisoners are past masters at faking symptoms that allow them to get all kinds of medication. To them, it's like taking a few beers. They take medication to change the routine, but it's dangerous. It makes you idiotic, and Quesnel must beware of this. He knows it."

To Quesnel, pills were a way of shifting the pain around. The routine of prison was weighing him down, and does so to this day. Now he tries to escape by studying, and finds freedom in books about algebra, in solving complicated problems. This is where he gets fulfilment. This is what allows him to keep hoping that he'll redeem himself, that he'll forever leave the world of crime and become an asset to society, as the lawyers say. He never wants to go back. He especially doesn't want to be another Mike Blass, an informant who served a nine-year sentence after committing a dozen murders. In 1997, while living in the Mauricie under a new name – Michel Simon – he murdered an antiquarian named Étienne Therrien and stole $5,000 from him. No one, except the police, knew that Blass was living in the Mauricie. Although they checked in on him once in a while, this didn't prevent him from killing again.

"Blass didn't take advantage of the exceptional opportunity he was given. Don't compare me to that guy! I've felt so good since I haven't had anything to blame myself for, and this is reason enough for me never to go back to crime. Blass seems beyond redemption. But I want to prove that an individual can mend his ways. That's my intention."

When defining happiness, Quesnel isn't very demanding. He wants a house, a wife, and a job. But even the woman who may share his life in the future won't know anything about his criminal past. Five years before his final release, he has already begun to reinvent the first thirty years of his life.

"I'm thinking a great deal about the version that'll be official. I'll need a story about having grown up in another country, where my parents are dead and where I have no living relatives. I won't take any risks, and no one will know anything. This is no laughing matter, since my life will depend on it. Some time ago, I met a beautiful woman in her forties. I have a picture of her, and we were in touch on a regular basis. Things were going a little too well. I was afraid that it was getting too serious and called off the relationship. She knew who I was. When I'm finally released, no one will know what's become of me. Not too many people are really able to keep a secret. I'm starting to prepare my new life. However, no one's told me what will happen on the day of my release. The authorities haven't told me because they don't want me to mention it to anyone. When I'm released, a car will be waiting for me. I'll get in and no one will ever see me again."

"An elaborate process has been planned," says Pierre Frenette. "A few months prior to his release, department officials who handle informants will get in touch with him. He'll be well prepared. Afterwards, when he has all the tools in hand and all the elements provided for in his contract, the rest will be up to him."

Serge Quesnel's father believes his son will pull through. He thinks that the Hells Angels he denounced will have other fish to fry and won't bother getting even with him. That's what he hopes.

"I believe those guys move on to other things very quickly. First of all, when he gets out, most of the guys he was with will no longer be there. Some will have grown old, others will have different occupations. I want him to go away, to leave Quebec. I want him to get a new identity and make a fresh start. It will be riskier if he stays here. Sometimes, I get the feeling he's worried about his future. I think he'll have to take a vacation before he decides what to do. I'd be afraid if he didn't find a stimulating environment. Serge often says, 'I don't want to work with a pickaxe and shovel.' The more I think about it, the less afraid I am. I tell myself, 'If he's stupid enough to botch things when he gets out, then he'll pay for it.'"

Frenette also believes the former killer for the Angels will pull through. "I think he has all the qualities needed to succeed in his new life. However, he'll have to avoid falling into drugs, and he'll have to stay in the shadows and be discreet. He'll have to avoid playing celebrity and stay quiet. If he does, the chances for his rehabilitation are excellent. Pit Caron is now out and doing very well. He'll succeed, and Quesnel probably will as well. He's smart and will pull through in the end. I'd be very surprised if he killed again."

And Quesnel himself seems confident. "I'm not scared of the bikers. Naturally, I won't take any risks, but the Angels will no longer be looking for me. I'll no longer be in the world of crime. That's settled for good. I'll make an honest living. I won't say in which field, but I'll find a job. I've spent my whole life fighting, but now I'll fight just for myself. I don't want any more problems or pressure. Once I regain my freedom, I won't want to lose it. Anyhow, the police will 'handle' me for the rest of my life. Sometimes, I have a nightmare. I break out of jail and, once out, I wonder about what I've just done and have regrets. That's significant."

Quesnel doesn't deny his past. He simply tries to understand what happened. "I'm not proud of having been with the Hells Angels. Nor am I proud of having betrayed them. The title of informant isn't honourable. However, I feel I found a way out. I'm now in a position to understand I wasn't really happy in that world. Being with the Angels is like a teenager's trip. You're brainwashed and things happen quickly. Biker gangs are like a cult. It's as though you're not aware of what's happening. Those guys worship the Hells Angels' symbol to an incredible extent. For them, death doesn't exist. They think they're immortal. There are signs in clubhouses that say that Angels never die, but go to hell to regroup. Many of them believe this. They're crazy!"

Quesnel stared into the distance, remaining quiet for a few seconds, then plunged back into his memories.

In January 2002, Quesnel told me that the Court of Appeal had ruled in favour of Coriace Landry in the suit he had filed against Quesnel. The court decided that Quesnel will have to pay for stabbing Landry at Donnacona, not the $16,300 he was originally ordered to pay but $20,000 more. With interest, Landry will get $55,000.

"This doesn't bother me," Quesnel says. "I'm not the one paying; it's the government. Not one penny will come out of my pocket. The authorities had promised to protect me against this kind of suit. It's lucky for me that two honest policemen signed a statement in my favour. Pierre Frenette and Tony Cannavino came to my rescue because officials were threatening to break the promise made to me. Journalists wrote that I'd be paying that sum, but that's not true, and I set the record straight with some of them."

In April 2002, I received a phone call from Quesnel. Things weren't going well. He was depressed and feeling like a caged animal. Being isolated was weighing him down more and more. His living conditions are poor and he was angry at the authorities. He said he didn't really want to sue the officials in charge of him again, mostly out of fear of reprisals. Soon he would be permitted temporary absences, and if he took on the authorities, they would put a spoke in that wheel. That's how things are done in prison.

"I can't stand this isolation any longer. I'll ask for a transfer. This is no way to live. I feel that the people I talk to are laughing at me. I'm at the end of my rope!"

From time to time, Quesnel gets desperate, and when he does, he threatens the authorities with new lawsuits. He has been in touch with a lawyer again and has sent him his file, which is huge and contains all his correspondence with the Public Security Department. Quesnel knows his rights and insists on them.

"The people asking that I become an honest citizen and respect the law should do the same. I honoured my contract with them, and they should reciprocate!"

Once again, as he's done throughout his life, Serge Quesnel is going for broke. He is ready to stick his neck out to get what he wants. But this time, he wants to do the right thing. The goal of his actions is to build, not destroy. Quesnel the criminal, killer, and informant will soon die, and the man who'll come out of jail will be a different man, facing a new life.

The QPF, for its part, feels that after all these years, the "Quesnel affair" has benefited the legal system and has saved the government hundreds of thousands of dollars in investigation fees. Thanks in part to Quesnel, many bikers have been sentenced: Mario Lussier, to twenty-five years; François Hinse, to four years; Mario Brouillette, to six years; Sylvain Thiffault, to two years; Clermont Carrier, to four years; and Claude Giguère, to two years. Rick Vallée is now behind bars. As for Melou Roy, he probably got the heaviest sentence following Quesnel's confession: his peers gave him the death penalty. Unless he went into exile. Forever.

Welcome to the world of bikers.

APPENDIX

1.

Contract signed June 14, 1995, between Serge Quesnel and four representatives from the Quebec government, which grants him several benefits.

Agreement between:
Serge Quesnel
And
Representatives from the Attorney General, the Public Security Department and the Quebec Police Force, hereinafter referred to as the Handling Committee.

Given the willingness displayed by Serge Quesnel to cooperate with the administration of justice, particularly by testifying in the proceedings related to the offences referred to in the present agreement.

1.   Serge Quesnel states:

a)   That between 1987 and 1994, he committed the crimes appearing on his police record, which is reproduced in Appendix A, and that he was sentenced by a court for each of those offences.

b)   That he was a party to the following offences in the file bearing number 200-01-003175-951:

1.   On or about January 29, 1995, in Grondines, district of Quebec, having caused the death of Jacques Ferland, thereby committing a murder in the first degree, a crime provided for in sections 235 and 21 of the Criminal Code.

2.   In January 1994 and January 1995, in Trois-Rivières, district of Trois-Rivières, and Grondines, district of Quebec City, having conspired, with Michel Caron, Louis Roy and Sylvain Thiffault, to commit a crime, namely: murder, thereby

committing the crime provided for in section 465 (1) c) of the Criminal Code.

3.   On or about January 29, 1995, in Grondines, district of Quebec City, using a firearm while planning a murder, thereby committing the crime provided for in section 85 (1) a) of the Criminal Code.

4.   On or about January 19, 1995, in Ancienne-Lorette, district of Quebec City, stole from Dominique Simard a Plymouth Sundance vehicle, whose value exceeded $5,000, thereby committing the crime provided for in sections 334 a) and 21 of the Criminal Code.

5.   In January 1995, in Saint-Augustin, district of Quebec City, stole from an unknown person a motor vehicle whose value exceeded $5,000, thereby committing the crime provided for in section 91 (1) a) of the Criminal Code.

6.   On or about January 29, 1995, in Grondines, district of Quebec City, having in his possession a restricted weapon, namely: a 9 mm pistol for which he didn't have a registration certificate, thereby

committing the crime provided for in section 91(1)
a) of the Criminal Code.

c) Having told Quebec Police Force officers about
his participation in the offences mentioned in subsection 1 b) in a statement reproduced in appendices B-1,
B-2 and B-3.

d) Having admitted to police authorities and to
the Handling Committee the crimes mentioned
in Appendix C for which he was never charged, in
exchange for the promise that these confessions could
never be used against him in any future proceedings.

e) Not having committed, to the best of his knowledge and recollection, other crimes in Canada.

f) Neither having been pressured nor threatened
by police, attorneys or other interveners to make a confession. To having been given no promises besides those
described hereafter.

2. Serge Quesnel undertakes to:

a) Reveal everything he knows to police investigators or the Attorney General's prosecutor assigned

to the file related to the crimes mentioned in the statements he made to Quebec Police Force officers between April 3 and June 14, 1995.

b)   Identify the place or places where any evidence can be found and, if necessary, accompany the police to the premises.

c)   Testify before Canadian courts as often as required with respect to the facts disclosed to Quebec Police Force officers between April 3 and June 14, 1995.

d)   Take all necessary and legal measures to avoid the disclosure of the arrangements made for his protection or that of a person in his care.

e)   To not commit crimes.

f)   To behave in accordance with the rules of the detention centre while he serves his sentence.

g)   To plead guilty, since he admits to committing the following offences:

– file 200-01-003175-951

1.   On or about January 29, 1995, in Grondines, district of Quebec, caused the death of Jacques Ferland, thereby committing a murder in the first degree, a crime provided for in sections 235 and 21 of the Criminal Code.

2.   In January 1994 and January 1995, in Trois-Rivières, district of Trois-Rivières, and Grondines, district of Quebec City, having conspired, with Michel Caron, Louis Roy and Sylvain Thiffault, to commit a crime, namely: murder, thereby committing the crime provided for in section 465 (1) c) of the Criminal Code.

3.   On or about January 29, 1995, in Grondines, district of Quebec City, using a firearm while planning a murder, thereby committing the crime provided for in section 85 (1) a) of the Criminal Code.

4.   On or about January 19, 1995, in Ancienne-Lorette, district of Quebec City, stole from Dominique Simard a Plymouth Sundance vehicle, whose value exceeded $5,000, thereby committing the crime provided for in sections 334 a) and 21 of the Criminal Code.

5.   On or about January 29, 1995, in Grondines, district of Quebec City, having in his possession a restricted weapon, namely: a 9 mm pistol for which he didn't have a registration certificate, thereby committing the crime provided for in section 91(1) a) of the Criminal Code.

– as well as to the following charges that are to be brought against him, namely:

the second-degree murders of Richard Delcourt, Richard Jobin, Martin Naud and Claude Rivard, conspiring to murder Gino Hallé, Jim Comeau, Stéphane Paré, Gilles Lambert, René Guillette, Luc Deschênes, Marcel Demers, Éric Pelletier, Denis Plante, Stéphane Trudel, Richard Pelletier, Harold Pelletier and Robert Dubuc, and assault causing bodily harm to Gaétan Gingras and Doris Laquerre.

3.   The Public Security Department (Security and Prevention Branch) undertakes to:

a)   Through the agency of the Quebec Police Force, give Serge Quesnel a weekly payment of $500 to cover his living expenses and those of his spouse, for the duration of his incarceration and for the first three years during which he will be on parole.

b)   Cover all living expenses incurred by Serge Quesnel between April 6, 1995, and this day, which is to say a sum of $4,832.58.

c)   Make the necessary requests to provide Serge Quesnel and his spouse a new legal identity when he is paroled, and cover all costs related to this change of identity and to the relocation of Quesnel and his spouse.

d)   Cover all costs related to the removal of his tattoos.

4.   The Quebec Police Force undertakes to:

a)   Take all the measures it considers necessary to ensure the protection of Serge Quesnel and his spouse, when required, and to do so until the end of the proceedings concerning the offences related to the facts disclosed to Quebec Police Force officers between April 3 and June 14, 1995.

b)   Provide transportation for Serge Quesnel when his presence is required either to prepare files or to testify before the court.

5.   The Correctional Services Branch undertakes to:

a)   Request from Correctional Services Canada a federal-provincial agreement allowing Serge Quesnel to serve his sentence in a provincial detention centre.

b)   Take all necessary measures to ensure his protection during his stay in a provincial detention centre specialized in dealing with informants, and to do so during the proceedings pertaining to the charges.

c)   When proceedings have ended, to relocate Mr. Quesnel in a provincial detention centre adapted to his situation and ensure his security.

d)   Inform the parole board about the appraisal report concerning Serge Quesnel, and about his co-operation with the administration of justice and his behaviour during detention.

e)   Allow Serge Quesnel to participate in provincial programs provided for by laws and regulations as long as he fulfills the eligibility criteria and that they do not jeopardize measures taken for his protection.

6.   Representatives from Quebec's Attorney General undertake to:

On a plea of guilty to the following offences:

–offences mentioned in subsection 29);

–charges that will be brought relating to the murders of Richard Delcourt, Richard Jobin, Martin Naud and Claude Rivard;

recommend to the court, following the imposition of a mandatory life sentence, that Serge Quesnel be eligible for parole following a 12-year detention period.

–   Moreover, following the charges that will be brought against Serge Quesnel, namely: conspiracies to murder Gino Hallé, Jim Comeau, Stéphane Paré, Gilles Lambert, René Guillette, Luc Deschênes, Marcel Demers, Éric Pelletier, Denis Plante, Stéphane Trudel, Richard Pelletier, Harold Pelletier and Robert Dubuc, and assault causing bodily harm to Gaétan Gingras and Doris Laquerre,

recommend the imposition of sentences to be served concurrently with this last sentence.

7.   If Serge Quesnel knowingly provides false information, makes a false testimony or commits a crime, he'll be prosecuted for any offence committed including perjury and obstruction of justice, in accordance with Canadian laws.

8.   Should Serge Quesnel knowingly not respect the commitments he has made in the present agreement, the signatories representing the Attorney General, the Department of Public Security and the Quebec Police Force reserve the right to unilaterally terminate all or part of the obligations mentioned in the present agreement.

9.   Serge Quesnel states that he does not wish to consult an attorney with respect to the present agreement, although the possibility of doing so was offered to him, and that he understands the terms and conditions.

10. The parties to the agreement acknowledge that:

The sentence is at the complete discretion of the court; the Crown, however, will highlight the cooperation of the accused, while respecting its obligation to provide the court with all elements relevant to the sentence.

All signatories to the agreement agree that it is final and that no other benefit has been granted by anyone and that no benefit which is not included in this agreement can be granted.

All signatories to the agreement acknowledge that no other agreement with Serge Quesnel exists besides the present document.

June 14, 1995

Mr. Louis Villemure
Representative of the
Attorney General

Mr. Serge Quesnel

Mr. Jean-Pierre Duchaine
Representative of the
Quebec Police Force

Mr. Arthur Fauteux
Representative of the
Public Security Department
Correctional Services Branch

Mr. Yvon Houle
Representative of the
Public Security Department
Security and Prevention Branch

2.

In March 2001, the government agreed to pay $30,000 to Serge Quesnel, because he was complaining that provisions of his contract related to detention conditions were not being respected. He was given assurances that he will not have to pay anything if he is again sentenced by a civil court.

Quebec City, March 6, 2001

Mr. Louis Riverin
Richard, Bérubé, Lévesque
3 Vallière Street, Suite 110
Quebec City, Quebec
G1K 6S9

Subject: Serge Quesnel
    vs.
    The Attorney General of Quebec
Your file no: Q-0001-1
Our file no: 99-05396

Dear Colleague,
    I hereby wish to confirm that an out-of-court settlement was reached with respect to the abovementioned file.

Department officials have authorized me to pay your client $30,000 including capital, interest and expenses without an admission of contractual or extra-contractual responsibility, but simply to avoid the lawsuit. Moreover, the department agrees to pay any additional sum for which your client may be sentenced to pay by the Court of Appeal in the file of Michel Landry vs. Serge Quesnel, plus additional fees for his lawyer, Mr. Posman.

As for the transfer to a provincial detention centre, steps will be taken as soon as possible and department officials still intend to respect the June 1995 agreement. The removal of tattoos will be performed according to a schedule respecting your client's medical file.

Legal and Legislative Affairs Branch
Legal Division
Saint-Laurent, Gagnon
300 Jean-Lesage Boulevard, Suite 103
Quebec City, Quebec
G1K 8K6

ACKNOWLEDGEMENTS

I would like to thank Carole for her constant support; Caroline and Yannick for their precious advice; Josée, Francis and Dominic for their help; my family for having encouraged me; and my work colleagues.

Thanks as well to Guy Samson from Correctional Services; to Pierre Frenette from the Quebec Police Force; to Guy Ouellet, a crime specialist; and to several employees from Quebec detention centres.